Survive the Drive

Survive the Drive

A Guide to Keeping Everyone on the Road Alive

2nd Edition

Tom Dingus

With Mindy Buchanan-King

VIRGINIA TECH TRANSPORTATION INSTITUTE
IN ASSOCIATION WITH

BLACKSBURG, VIRGINIA

Second edition first published 2020 by Virginia Tech Transportation Institute in association with Virginia Tech Publishing

Virginia Tech Transportation Institute
3500 Transportation Research Plaza
Blacksburg, VA 24061

Virginia Tech Publishing
Virginia Tech University Libraries
560 Drillfield Drive
Blacksburg, VA 24061

Every effort has been made to contact and acknowledge copyright owners, but the authors would be pleased to have any errors or omissions brought to their attention so that corrections may be published in future editions.

Series enumeration supplied by publisher.
ISBN: 978-1-949373-24-0 (epub)
ISBN: 978-1-949373-25-7 (paperback)
ISBN: 978-1-949373-26-4 (pdf)

DOI: https://doi.org/10.21061/survive-the-drive/
Cover art by Alex Parrish

Contents

Preface

Driving is risky business. Only cancer, heart attacks, and strokes cause more unintentional deaths among the general population. Driving is the leading cause of unintentional death for those between the ages of 4 and 34.

Unlike cancer, heart attacks, and strokes, driving does not discriminate by age. More than 37,000 deaths occur each year from crashes on US highways. Many of these crash victims are teenagers or young adults according to the National Highway Traffic Safety Administration (NHTSA) Fatality Analysis Reporting System (commonly referred to in our industry as FARS). In fact, all you have to do is look at the 2016 NHTSA *Summary of Motor Vehicle Crashes* fact sheet—which is based on FARS information—for a sobering reminder of the risks that drivers face, from more than 3.14 million injuries sustained during the year to nearly 11,000 fatalities due to alcohol-impaired driving.

Maybe the risk of experiencing a fatal or disabling crash looks, relatively speaking, pretty low. After all, there are more than 320 million people in the US alone, 225 million of whom are licensed drivers. Let's put your crash risk into perspective, though: by far, more people die from driving than from many of the recreational activities we think of as "dangerous." The rates in the table below have been corrected for the number of participants.

Fatality rate, per 100,000 participants

Skiing/snowboarding	0.4
Hunting	0.7
White-water kayaking	2.9
Ice, snow, or rock climbing	3.2
Scuba diving	3.5
Recreational boating	6.5
Driving	15.2

As the numbers show, you are much more likely to die in a car crash than you are to die participating in any of the other activities that may be characterized as "extreme" or "risky." Take, for instance, white-water kayaking. Out of

100,000 folks who kayak, an average of 2.9 people die in a given year while kayaking. What this tells us is that our perception of risk is not very accurate when it comes to driving.

There's another important takeaway from these statistics. Why do you think that driving and recreational boating top the list? Well, one big factor is alcohol (a topic for later), which gets back to the risk-perception issue. Ask yourself, How many people ice climb or scuba dive drunk? Not very many. Why? Because participants in these sports understand (and estimate pretty well) the risks. Driving is risky too, but we aren't very good at assessing that risk. But if we understand the risk and learn how to reduce that risk, we can increase our odds of survival a great deal.

Understanding Your Risk: An Easy Math Lesson

Throughout the book I will be giving you estimates of the odds associated with certain aspects of driving—aspects ranging from distraction (think texting) to driving under the influence of alcohol. The concept of "odds" is not difficult to grasp. In essence, odds are the likelihood—or risk—of something happening. For our purposes, that something is a crash, and most often the odds I give you will tell you how much risk you face of being in a crash under certain conditions (whatever those conditions might be) compared to the *ideal* conditions of driving on dry roads in daylight while alert, attentive, and unimpaired (sober). If the odds I give you are not based on that comparison, I will let you know. Therefore, if I tell you that your odds of being in a crash are 1.0, this means that you would have exactly the same risk if you were driving under the ideal circumstances described above. If the odds are 1.3, you are about 30 percent more likely to crash than if you were driving under ideal conditions; if the odds are 2.0, then you are twice as likely to crash; if the odds are 6.0, then you are six times, or 600 percent, as likely to crash, and so on.

I bring up the distinction between percentages and odds because people, including the media, often confuse them. For example, the Virginia Tech Transportation Institute (VTTI), of which I am director, did an analysis that showed texting and driving for heavy-truck drivers increased the risk of a safety-critical event (that is, a crash, near crash, minor collision, etc.) by 23 times. Unfortunately, some media sources then erroneously reported that texting while driving increases your risk by 23 percent. That is a *huge* difference between our study results and what was reported. A few key points got lost in translation: (1) the 23-times statistic applies to heavy trucks, not to all vehicles, and (2) the increased crash risk in terms of percentages is not 23 percent; it is 2,300 percent! Sometimes throughout this book, I have to use percentages to explain the risk because I don't have strong enough data to calculate the odds. For example, you need numbers like how many people *didn't* crash while driving on icy roads to calculate the odds of crashing on ice, which is sometimes hard to pinpoint. Therefore, you will see statements such as "increases fatal crash risk by 60 percent." Just remember that this number is not exactly the same as odds of 1.6. In general terms, though, the two convey roughly the same amount of risk.

There are times that the odds can be less than 1.0. In these cases, there exists what we refer to as a "protective effect." In other words, you have *reduced* your odds of a crash. A great example is the presence of passengers. If you are an adult (we will talk about teens later), the odds of you having a crash are about 0.5 when you are traveling with passengers relative to when you drive alone. Therefore, as an adult, you are twice as safe when passengers are present. We are not exactly sure why there is a reduced risk of a crash in this scenario, but a few factors are certainly at play. First, adults tend to drive more conservatively when passengers are present. Second, passengers probably help keep the driver alert. And third, the passengers serve as another set of eyes to spot hazards. My wife is a very good "crash avoidance system" in this regard, letting me know in no uncertain terms when I have missed or underestimated a potential hazard.

When I assess the risk of a crash in terms of odds or percentages, I am usually drawing on scientific research. Most of the time there are scientific papers or reports to back up the risk odds or percentages, either written by myself or with coauthors or by esteemed colleagues in the field. (References to such research are found at the end of the book, should you want to delve into the scientific details.) In cases where the published research may be thin or inadequate, I will estimate odds or percentages based on my own expertise gained from more than 35 years of research experience in the field. I am providing odds and percentage estimates so that you can understand the crash risks and decide accordingly how best to reduce your personal odds and those of your kids, parents, friends, or spouse. My hope, of course, is that you will heed the advice in this book so that your odds of suffering a serious crash will be cut in half.

The Data Used

The odds and percentages provided throughout this book are almost exclusively based on studies conducted in actual field settings or come from databases derived from actual crashes. While laboratory and simulation studies have their benefits, the very fact that they take place in closed environments limits our ability to estimate crash risk from them. There are several large crash databases that are developed and stored by NHTSA. The sources of these data are primarily police reports filled out by investigating officers after a crash. Other databases are developed through more in-depth analyses conducted by trained crash investigators. These databases are powerful tools that help us understand much about crash factors, and they are referenced throughout this book.

What is very hard, or sometimes even impossible, to gauge using post-crash investigations is what happened in the seconds leading up to a crash. This timeframe is critical for determining such factors as driver drowsiness, distraction, error, aggressive driving, and road conditions. Crash investigation reports are only as good as the information collected by the investigator, and the majority of that information comes from interviewing those involved in the crash. However, following a crash, drivers and passengers may be dead, injured, or dazed or may not have been looking in the right direction, may not remember what occurred, or may be trying to hide something. This is why VTTI developed the naturalistic driving study research method some 20 years ago.

In the late 1990s I began collaborating with a friend and colleague named Mike Goodman from NHTSA on what would become the first large-scale naturalistic driving study. The study used 100 cars traveling on the road for 13 months. A brilliant team of VTTI hardware and software engineers and fellow researchers helped us create and define the concept behind naturalistic driving studies. We determined that we needed more real-world data to explain why people crashed. We needed data from the vehicles themselves to determine what was happening at the time of a safety-critical event—that is, a crash, near crash, minor collision, etc. We also needed video to corroborate what was happening with the vehicle. For instance, if the car experienced a sudden deceleration, we needed visuals to determine why the driver slammed on the brakes. Was the driver distracted? Fatigued? Impaired? To solve this problem, we developed special instrumentation (including an inconspicuous suite of cameras, sensors, and radar) along with increasingly sophisticated data acquisition systems (DASs). Andy Petersen and his team at the Center for Technology Development design and build all the DASs used in VTTI naturalistic driving studies.

The "naturalistic driving study research method" was pioneered some 20 years ago by VTTI. A VTTI-developed data acquisition system, dubbed the MiniDAS.

Only volunteers are used for our naturalistic driving studies; they receive no training and no directions from VTTI researchers. Their only task is to drive as they normally do. For nearly two decades, we have equipped more than 4,000 vehicles to collect what now stands at more than 2,000,000 hours of continuous naturalistic driving data. We have also captured nearly 2,000 crashes (and counting) and more than 10,000 near crashes as part of this data-acquisition effort. This unique data resource is continually tapped by federal transportation agencies, departments of transportation, even major automobile manufacturers and suppliers. It is the cornerstone of our primary goal at VTTI: to save lives.

One more point about odds. You will notice that none of the odds you see in this book are zero. Even when you have done everything you can to be safer or to create a protective effect (that is, create an environment where your odds of being in a crash are less than 1.0), *you are still at some risk.*

An example screenshot illustrating the camera views captured by our data acquisition systems.

The only way to eliminate your odds of being killed or injured in a crash while driving is to not drive! This is the concept of exposure. If you drive less, take public transit more, drive in better weather, and drive on safer roads, you reduce your risk by reducing your exposure. This will be an important concept throughout this book, and it is something that you should consider as you decide whether—and how—to get from point A to point B. There are a few simple alternative ways to reduce your exposure and the exposure of others without having to stay home all the time:

1. ***Get out of the driver's seat and save the planet while saving yourself.***
   One way to manage your risk is to take more public transit. A transit bus is safer than a car. They have significant mass; they are easy to see; and in most cases they are operated by alert, sober, and attentive drivers. It is a rare event when a driver of this type of heavy vehicle falls asleep at the wheel or is distracted to the point of causing a crash involving many people.

2. **Put your kids on the school bus, go home, and have another cup of coffee.** From a transportation perspective, there really are fewer places safer for your kids than a school bus. School buses have large mass; they are very noticeable given that they are giant orange vehicles that feature flashing lights; and like all buses, they are almost always operated by trained, sober, and reasonably alert drivers. Having said that, it is important to reinforce with your kids how to enter and exit the bus, because these are the moments when almost all the risks occur for kids on school buses.

From this point forward, you will never see me use the word *accident* again in the book. I used to charge students in my transportation safety course 25 cents every time they uttered the word in class. By the end of the semester, we had enough money for pizza. Why did I put them through this? Because *accident* implies an unfortunate event that can't be controlled or managed; an accident is something that just happens. However, as you will read in this book, you have significant control over your risk while driving. If these risks are properly managed, you can avoid many, many crashes. You also have the capability to manage the potential consequences for those cases during which a crash cannot be avoided. For instance, you can choose a safe vehicle, wear personal protective gear that includes a seat belt, or wear a bicycle or motorcycle helmet if you are of the two- or three-wheel crowd. All these choices affect how a crash will impact your life, or how the impact will crash your life, as the case may be.

So, read on and learn how to best control your driving situation, manage your risk, and avoid or lessen the probability or severity of a *crash*! But keep in mind that crashes do happen—about 11 million per year in the United States. Even if you do everything right, you may get in a crash. Therefore, it is just as important to make sure that if someone crashes into you, you have done everything you can not only to survive but to walk away.

Acknowledgments

I have been extremely fortunate. I have a great and supportive family that appears in numerous stories within these pages. I have wonderful friends who are like family, great colleagues and mentors who are some of my best friends, and students who have been my best teachers. The greatest part, though, is that most of them—and, certainly, all the ones who appear in this book—fall in at least two of those categories. We have been on a long journey together, sometimes deliberate and sometimes random, and that journey has allowed us to do a great thing: save people from needless injury and death due to car crashes. How could a life and a life's work be any better than that?

Abbreviations

AAA	American Automobile Association
ABS	anti-lock brake systems
AEB	automatic emergency braking
BAC	blood alcohol content
CDC	Centers for Disease Control and Prevention
DAS	data acquisition system
ESC	electronic stability control
FARS	Fatality Analysis Reporting System
FHWA	Federal Highway Administration
FMCSA	Federal Motor Carrier Safety Administration
GDL	graduated driver's licensing
IIHS	Insurance Institute for Highway Safety
NHTSA	National Highway Traffic Safety Administration
NIH	National Institutes of Health
SAE	Society for Automotive Engineers
VTTI	Virginia Tech Transportation Institute

1. Physics 101

Know Your Car and Your Options

The very first lesson to remember while driving is that roadways are full of objects of unusual size and weight (mass) moving at high rates of speed (acceleration). This can create tremendous forces, particularly in a crash. If you took physics in high school, this is what your physics teacher tried to teach you:

Force = Mass x Acceleration, or F = MA.

Roadways are full of objects of varying mass traveling at high rates of speed. In a potential crash situation, it is always better to be in a vehicle of high rather than low mass.

What does this mean? Well, if you want to increase your chances of survival during a crash, slower speeds are better (although, as I will discuss later, going too slow can also create force in a crash). Avoiding objects of increased mass will also reduce the potential for high forces and lessen the severity of crashes. The easiest lesson to learn here is to *stay away from trucks* ... unless, of course, you are a truck driver. We'll talk in more detail about this point later because I can't emphasize it enough.

A side note to the F = MA lesson is that it is always better to be on the high-mass side rather than the low-mass side of any crash. Therefore, if you find yourself in a crash situation, you want to be the one exerting most of the force as opposed to absorbing most of the force. Think of a head-on crash between a locomotive and a car traveling at equal speeds. While the train engineer will barely feel the impact, the car driver will certainly feel the impact.

Based on this lesson, here are two thoughts to bear in mind when choosing a vehicle:

1. **If you have a choice, go with the bigger car.** I hesitate to say this, but all things considered, the bigger the car, the more likely you are to survive a serious crash. Of course, there are a lot of practical trade-offs to this alternative, including increased cost for gas and a substantial negative environmental impact. Be that as it may, big cars generally help you survive a crash more effectively than small cars because they weigh more and typically sit up higher so that more of the forces are transmitted through the body of the car.
2. **Newer is better.** Despite what I just said about mass (that is, the bigger, the better), the newer the car, the safer the car. And in general the more expensive the car model, the safer the car. If you find yourself saying, "Wow, rich people have the capability to be safer than poor people," you are absolutely (and unfortunately) right. However, there is good news. Unlike many aspects of income inequality, the gap regarding the ability to purchase a safe car has been narrowing for a number of years. In fact, newer low-cost cars can be very safe. The key is to look at the government safety ratings, but be aware that the scales are different for different-sized cars (*mass!*). Therefore, I recommend that you put yourself and your family in the safest car that you can, given all the trade-offs above.

Our friends at the Insurance Institute for Highway Safety (IIHS) conduct studies periodically that determine the number of fatal crashes per million vehicles of a particular model on the road. These studies include a variety of makes and models. Recent IIHS studies have found that new vehicles are improving greatly in crashworthiness and even crash-avoidance technology, with fatality rates overall dropping with each model year. With the information above, you can guess which kinds of vehicles are generally the safest: those that are bigger and heavier and newer with more safety features. Vehicles that sit up higher also translate to increased safety because most, if not all, of the force will be transmitted through the entire body in this type of vehicle, regardless of the height of whatever you hit. What this all means is that SUVs dominate the list, with a minivan or two sprinkled in. At the bottom of the list are compacts and subcompacts, even those that received a five-star safety rating from IIHS.

This is all good information, and you should pay attention to it. However, you should be careful in how you interpret the results. For example, the "best" vehicles are generally not those driven by younger drivers, are not purchased by car enthusiasts because they are bigger, and tend to be used more by families. Thus, they are driven by folks who aren't as likely to crash. It should also be noted that the IIHS data are not corrected for miles driven. For example, if you drive a lot of miles, you may tend to drive a smaller, more fuel-efficient car.

Despite the limitations of the IIHS data, the underlying trends are undeniable. For example, 11 of the vehicles listed under the 2014 model year category of the IIHS results had *zero* fatalities per million vehicles on the road. Even 10 years ago, there wasn't one vehicle on that list with a zero fatality rating per million vehicles.

However, don't be overconfident! Before you purchase one of these vehicles and start feeling invincible on the road, keep in mind that, according to NHTSA, the crash fatality rate increased in the US in 2012 for the first time in a number of years and then again in 2015 and 2016. In other words, we have a long way to go till driving fatalities seriously approach zero. Therefore, it's imperative to keep reading this book!

Safety Factors beyond Weight ... and My 1971 VW Bus

The modern car is an amazing feat of engineering. In addition to the obvious performance and luxury features, newer vehicles are designed to transmit the force of a crash around the passenger compartment and provide "landing surfaces" (airbags). Everything from collapsible steering columns to shatter-proof glass, crumple zones, seat belt tensioners, and up to 11 airbags make the cars of today much, much safer than cars of even the recent past. All these factors minimize the damage to drivers and passengers. This ability to essentially protect the driver and passengers during a crash is known as the vehicle's crashworthiness.

By contrast, let's consider my 1971 VW bus. While driving my bus, my feet were essentially inches away from the front bumper. My midsection was mere inches from the steering wheel. The only redeeming fact in that regard was that the wheel made for a great place to hang on in a rollover crash. If you drove this bus and were concerned about crashworthiness, you mounted the spare tire on the front to provide more cushion in case of a frontal collision. There were no airbags, no door impact beams, and no heat to speak of. Horsepower in these vehicles was pretty nonexistent, which is probably why many of us of a certain generation are still alive today.

Cars have come a long way from the VWs I owned in the 1970s.

Since my '71 VW, cars have come a long way and vary significantly. We've talked about size and weight changes, but there are also pretty big differences between makes and models of the same relative weight and the same year of manufacture. Do yourself and your family a favor and look at the NHTSA 5-Star Safety Ratings and the IIHS Top Safety ratings. With these resources you can find plenty of helpful information about the crashworthiness of almost any car—new or used—that you may want to buy.

I was fortunate enough to be able to buy my kids newer cars. (Technically, I paid half and they paid the other half with money they saved or received over the years, primarily from their grandparents.) I told them they could get any car they wanted, as long as it was a Honda Civic. There are plenty of good choices out there, and while the Civic doesn't have a lot of mass, it does consistently have high safety ratings from both NHTSA and IIHS. The Civic is also reliable, environmentally friendly, economical, and relatively inexpensive, and it holds its value. It has a full complement of airbags, low horsepower (important!), and a feature I *really* like: the seat belt reminder never quits. In other words, the car pings a warning every mile forever and ever if you don't wear your seat belt. I essentially knew that my kids would always be belted.

My son, Chris, just recently sold his 2007 Civic with more than 150,000 miles on it, and my daughter, Emily, no longer has her 2008 Civic. After my wife and I sent Emily away to college, we went on a month-long trip to Australia and New Zealand to give some lectures about distracted driving. While we were gone, Emily came home from college during Labor Day to see friends. On her way back to college, she was driving in a torrential rainstorm (1.5 inches per hour), hydroplaned at the bottom of a big hill, spun around at highway speeds, and hit the guardrail. Three airbags deployed; she hit her head on the front airbag and the side-curtain airbag hard enough to break her glasses and suffer a concussion. I got a call in New Zealand at 4:00 a.m. that started with the words "Don't freak out."

What do you think would have happened had she not had a car with airbags? Or if she had been unbelted and out of her normal driving position when the airbags deployed? The potential was certainly there for permanent brain injury, or worse. Then I really would have freaked out.

2. Simple Ways to Reduce Your Risk

Sound bites are one of the banes of modern life. This seems to be particularly true when it comes to driving safety. You often hear news reports that claim one cause for a crash, such as, "A driver, under the influence of alcohol, hit a cyclist." However, crashes themselves–and the degree to which those involved are injured–are rarely the result of a single factor. Inevitably, there are several contributing factors at play: the driver may have been using a cell phone, the crash may have occurred at night, the cyclist may have been wearing dark clothing with minimal or no reflectors, and/or the driver may have had a blood alcohol content below the legal limit. These multiple factors are known as the interaction between causal (primary) and contributing (secondary) factors.

How a Crash Is Like Baking a Cake

One thing you will notice as you read this book is that if you add up all the percentages of crash risk factors (such as alcohol, distracted driving, aggressive driving, drowsy driving), you will be way over 100 percent. You may wonder how this can be. It's because three or four factors often interact to cause a single crash.

One can think about this phenomenon like a recipe–let's say it's a recipe for a birthday cake. Each ingredient in this figurative birthday cake represents a factor that can contribute to a crash. A crash happens when all the ingredients are present to complete the "mix." Sometimes, one or two ingredients are missing, so you can't make the cake. One real-world example of a key ingredient is the act of taking your eyes off of the road to glance at something, otherwise known as distracted driving.

Distraction becomes the key ingredient in this scenario. But if one or more other ingredients aren't present–say, the car in front of you doesn't brake unexpectedly while you are distracted–then a crash won't occur. It's when you have three or four factors working against you while driving that you typically have a crash. Therefore, one way to think about how to avoid crashes is to make sure that you keep one or more of the key ingredients, like distraction, out of the cake recipe.

Crashes are not usually caused by a single factor; they happen when multiple factors are present to complete the "mix," like ingredients in a birthday cake.

In addition to the crash's causal and contributing factors, there are other ingredients that determine whether you are injured and to what extent. Let's think of these ingredients as the proverbial icing on the cake. These ingredients include such factors as how well your vehicle is designed to protect you during a crash (also known as crashworthiness), whether or not you're wearing a seat belt, and the presence of heavy, loose objects in the vehicle that could become dangerous projectiles during a crash.

The following is an example from my own history to illustrate this recipe simile.

My friend Rick left our home in Fairborn, Ohio, after graduating from Wright State University to attend graduate school at the University of Illinois at Urbana-Champaign. During Rick's semester break, our friend Bob, (another) Rick, and I hopped into my 1973 VW bus (not to be confused with my '71 VW bus) and headed bravely across Indiana to visit him and check out this town in Illinois. How can you go wrong when your college buddy moves to a town called Champaign?

As we were known to do, we had a spirited weekend—all the while, something called the Blizzard of '78 started happening right outside our door. Of course, we barely noticed the blizzard. When the end of the weekend arrived, we managed to dig out the bus and start the return trip east, moving at a snail's pace because of the snow. My bus had a terrible heater, so Bob brought along a portable propane heater. Rick was sitting cross-legged with his shoes off. In the back of the bus (which, of course, had no trunk) we had stashed several unopened cases of beer and bottles of liquor that we had bought in Illinois. (Hey, it was cheaper there.)

Driving in snow and ice requires that we adapt accordingly to avoid losing control of our cars, as happened on this Alabama road in 2017.

As we traveled along, moving out of Illinois and into Indiana, the road conditions slowly improved. Our speed gradually crept from 25 mph to 35 mph, 45 mph, and eventually 55 mph because the roads were plowed and salted. I was in a hurry to get home because I had a busy week of tests and studying ahead. We were feeling really good about the trip back home ... until we passed under an overpass that also happened to be a county line. It turned out that the roads in Indiana were maintained county by county. Unfortunately, the county into which we had crossed had not yet extended its road maintenance onto I-70.

As we crossed the line, the interstate was covered in sheer ice. Cars were scattered everywhere in both ditches. Our VW bus didn't fare any better. We started slipping and spun around backwards. My friend Rick said the most intelligent thing I had heard in a while: "Hold on!" We hit the median and the bus rolled over 1.75 times. I had a death grip on the steering wheel because we didn't have seat belts on. I distinctly remember the windshield popping out on the first rollover. Bob wrestled a time or two with his heater.

Hydroplaning is tested at the VTTI-affiliated Global Center for Automotive Performance Simulation (GCAPS).

When it was all over, my bus looked like an A-frame. There were broken beer bottles everywhere, and we were soaked in beer. It was 20 degrees outside. Rick had a chipped tooth and never found his shoes. Bob had a cut over his eye, but that was (thankfully) the extent of the bodily damage incurred. No one was cut from all the broken glass. There was one unbroken bottle, a fifth of Jack Daniel's, which had flown between Rick and me and through the windshield, landing about 20 feet in front of the bus. Cars going the opposite way had already pulled over, and a state patrolman followed almost instantly. We grabbed our duffel bags. I talked to the patrolman, who was very sympathetic even though I was soaked in beer, probably because it was 9:30 a.m. and he had likely received 20 other calls about more crashes on the interstate. I filled out the paperwork, the officer called a tow truck, and he gave us a ride to the Greyhound bus station. We had a couple of hours to wait for our bus, which gave me plenty of time to think about what we had just been through. I remember saying to Bob, "Man, I almost killed us." To which he replied, "But you didn't. We got lucky." I repeated what I had just said, and he just grabbed my shoulder and handed me the bottle of Jack Daniel's. By the time we got back to Ohio, the Jack Daniel's was gone.

From that point on, every time Rick's dad saw me, he asked, "You keepin' the shiny side up these days?" "Keeping the shiny side up" meant keeping my vehicle right-side up, which was his way of asking if I was staying safe. All in all, the incident was a perfect example of my cake metaphor. All the ingredients were present to make the cake: terrible roads; unexpected black ice; an overconfident, young male driver; crashworthiness and vehicle handling near zero; and heavy, loose, dangerous objects. One more ingredient—such as a bottle flying in the wrong place; our vehicle encountering a guardrail, another car, or a steep embankment; or our bus crossing over into oncoming traffic—and I wouldn't be writing this book.

What would have helped us in our situation? For starters, our heavy, dangerous objects could have been securely stowed (or placed in a trunk if the vehicle had one). We could have traveled in a vehicle with a lower center of gravity and better heat. We definitely should have been wearing our seat belts. The county in which the crash occurred could have implemented better road maintenance or warnings. Most of all, though, I needed to better understand the risks I faced as a driver and to adapt to the conditions appropriately. When driving, you definitely *don't* want to have your cake and eat it too.

Now for a few simple tips to reduce your risk while driving. While they may seem like no-brainers, they can easily be forgotten in the routine of daily driving. Remembering to heed them might just ensure that at least one of the basic ingredients of a crash is missing so that the proverbial cake never gets made.

Seat Belts: They May Seem Like a Nuisance, but Wear Them Anyway!

Crashes can be exceptionally violent events with tremendous accelerations and forces applied in virtually any direction. However, the good news is that you have seat belts. This can't be stressed enough: there is no better option to protect yourself in a crash than to wear a seat belt. We have all heard it for years, but the following are facts:

- **You double your odds (odds = 2.0) of an injury or fatality in a crash if you aren't wearing a seat belt.**
- **For a head-on crash, of which there are approximately 10,000 each year, you are five times more likely to walk away without a serious injury or fatality if you have an airbag and are wearing a seat belt.**

Essentially, your odds are 0.2 if you are involved in a head-on crash but have an airbag *and* wear your seat belt. That's a tremendous protective effect. However, the *and* part is important. Airbags can actually cause injuries in crashes in which the driver is unbelted and out of the normal driving position. And let's face it—airbags aren't going to be much help if a driver is unbelted and is ejected out of his or her vehicle during a rollover crash.

The good news is that most of us wear seat belts, and the number of those wearing seat belts in the US is increasing each year. The national seat belt use rate is about 90 percent. According to 2017 statistics, Georgia wins the driving safety award for the highest seat belt use within the US with a rate of 97.1 percent. New Hampshire has the lowest rate, 67.6 percent, which makes sense, as it is the one state that has no seat belt law (think Live Free and Die … whoops, I mean Live Free *or* Die).

In big round numbers, the seat belt use rate is about 5 percent lower for males (testosterone enables them to fend off the impact of airbags), 14 percent lower for rural states (which is ironic since rollover crashes are more common in such locations), and 9 percent lower for states with secondary seat belt laws (that is, you can't get pulled over just because you're not wearing your seat belt) or no seat belt law at all (New Hampshire).

Another good reason to wear a seat belt was demonstrated by my friend Rick. I was driving my '71 VW bus one evening on the way to buy beer. Rick was sitting sideways in the passenger seat, leaning against his door. As I made a sweeping left-hand turn through the near-empty parking lot, the passenger-side door popped open and Rick flew out, did a backwards roll, and landed on his feet. Luckily, he only ended up with a few minor bruises. He had been holding a glass bottle in his hand when he fell out of the car, and what was left of the bottle was still in his hand.

Here is some cheap, but effective, advice regarding seat belt use: if you are a lawmaker, pass a primary seat belt law for both front- and rear-seat occupants if your state doesn't have such a law. You will save a lot of lives and be a hero, honest. If you are a police officer or supervisor of police officers, the enforcement of whatever laws are on the books helps significantly. I know it is a hard law to enforce, but there are ways to do it. Hawaii or Georgia may be good places to look for ideas since they have higher compliance rates.

Pay Special Attention to the Kids—They Need You

My wife Melissa and I were driving around town a few years ago. Melissa and I met in graduate school, and we both continue to work at VTTI in driving safety. On this particular day we pulled up to a stoplight, and beside us was a pickup truck with what appeared to be a four-year-old child standing in the front passenger seat and leaning over the dashboard. It was all I could do to keep Melissa from jumping out of the car, running over, and "educating" the driver (in live traffic) about the dangers of not having your kid restrained properly. If a relatively minor (non-injurious) front-end crash had occurred or if a rear-end crash had happened in which a car hit the stopped pickup from behind and forced the pickup to hit a vehicle in front, the passenger-side airbag would have deployed. In such a case, the kid could have easily been killed—maybe even launched through the back window—in a situation where no injury should have occurred.

When it comes to the children in your lives, child passenger safety laws vary state by state (AAA has some good resources about laws across each state in the US; see References at the end of this book for more information). You would think buckling up your child when going for a drive would be a no-brainer nowadays, but the Centers for Disease Control and Prevention (CDC) recently reported that in a one-year span more than 618,000 children aged 0–12 used no safety/booster seat or seat belt at least some of the time while riding. Of those aged 12 and younger who died in a crash, 35 *percent were unrestrained.*

It is sad that this has to be written, but make sure your child is safely restrained in a vehicle—in *any* vehicle, not just yours. We know at VTTI that rideshare services like Uber and Lyft are popular, so some of our researchers looked at child safety-seat use with such services. Data analysis results based on focus groups of parent riders and rideshare drivers found that only one-half of parents currently provide a personal safety seat while using a rideshare service, though most parents said they would feel comfortable using the service with their child if the company provided a child safety seat and the driver had basic training in child passenger safety. Overall, most rideshare drivers and parent riders believe child passenger safety laws should apply to rideshare services, yet regulations can be very ambiguous. While 34 states exempt taxis and/or for-hire vehicles from their child-restraint laws (clearly a mistake for you legislators who are reading this), where rideshare services fit in the picture is less clear. Good ol' Georgia wins here again, being the only state to make a legislative distinction between ridesharing and taxi/for-hire vehicles. While the latter are excluded from state child-restraint laws, rideshare services are explicitly included.

Moreover, you want to ensure your child is restrained *correctly.* NHTSA found that nearly 50 percent of child safety seats were misused (by placing the child safety seat in the front passenger seat of the vehicle, failing to secure the child safety seat on a vehicle seat, using an aftermarket belt tightener, etc.) in such a way that the benefits of the seats were negated. NHTSA has a great brochure called *Keeping Kids Safe: A Parent's Guide to Protecting Children in and around Cars* (https://bit.ly/2EE5w9l) to help guardians navigate the proper way to install a child safety seat as well as to select the appropriate seats (rear-facing, forward-facing, booster) to use at each stage of a child's development. If you need help ensuring your child's safety seat is installed correctly, please check with your local fire or police station; police officers or firefighters should be able to show you for free how to properly install the seat.

In essence, if you are a driver, husband, wife, parent, or child, make sure *everyone* wears seat belts for even the shortest trip. You will likely get into a couple of crashes in your lifetime, and seat belts really, really, really could save your life. Seat belts also keep you from getting into an unintentional wrestling match with everyone else in your car during a crash. While his weight may not seem important while taking a leisurely stroll or going to the movies, having your 200-pound husband flying at you out of control in a car during a crash can cause serious injury. So, either make him wear his seat belt or put him on a serious diet.

According to the National Highway Traffic Safety Administration, nearly 50 percent of child safety seats are misused. Make sure your child is safely and correctly restrained in your vehicle.

Speaking of unbelted mammals of large size traveling in a car ...

Remember Your Pets—They Are Passengers Like You

I was riding along with my friend Mark one day on our way to a ski trip in Colorado. The road was icy, and my brakes were not working so well (pretty spongy) in my old '66 Baja Bug. However, being undaunted and 20 years old, we pressed ahead through the snow in search of slopes. Our skis were bungee-corded relatively securely to a roof rack on top. My malamute, Wolf, was riding along in the back seat. Wolf was a *big dog*.

As we were traveling along, the car in front of us stopped suddenly and we slammed into it. Even with no shoulder belt (that particular car model only had lap belts), I would have been able to keep my face from hitting the steering wheel except for—you guessed it—Wolf slamming into the back of my seat. The driver seat had no seatback lock lever or headrest, which meant I slammed my face into the steering wheel anyway. If that wasn't bad enough, Wolf came over the top of the seat and landed on top of me, creating (luckily) only a few bruises and cuts. He also popped out the front windshield, which made for a very cold ride home. To add insult to (literally) injury, Wolf, although relatively unscathed, was very scared and proceeded to pee all over me while he struggled to find his footing. Since the Baja had a fiberglass front and was lightweight, the impact itself caused little damage to the car in front of us. However, our roof rack broke loose and slid up and over the car in front, peeling paint off that car from the trunk to the hood.

Tom and Wolf as a puppy; from the author's personal photo collection

The moral of the story is to think of your pets, and anything else heavy in your car, as potential projectiles heading straight for you—or rolling around with you—in a crash. There are a variety of products available to belt your dog in the back seat, or there are dividers that separate you from your pet. It's better for them and it's better for you to use such products.

And keep your gold bars or dumbbells (or sledgehammers, chainsaws, and toolboxes) in the trunk!

Speed(ing) Kills

Anyone who has studied driving safety for a long time will tell you the factors that most often contribute to fatal crashes: booze, speed, and unused seat belts. (More recently, driver distraction has been added to the list.) Here are some facts to consider regarding speed. **In general, speeding more than 10 mph over the speed limit or driving too fast for conditions increases your odds of being in a crash by *about* 12 *times* (odds = 12.0).**

According to NHTSA, in 2016 nearly 20 percent of drivers involved in fatal crashes were speeding, and the total number of fatalities involving speeding increased by nearly 5 percent over the previous year. It's really easy to speed in a modern car. Even economy vehicles can go very fast, much faster than is safe or legal. I will talk at some length about alcohol and other types of impairment later in this book, but it should be emphasized up front that alcohol impacts both your driving performance and your driving behavior. Alcohol can also impact a driver's judgment, leading to traveling at high speeds and not wearing seat belts.

Consider this: if you are drunk at the legal blood alcohol content limit (BAC = 0.08 percent), you are 2.5 *times more likely* (odds = 2.5) to die while speeding than if you are sober.Speeding increases your crash risk for a number of reasons. These include a greater chance of losing control of the vehicle, creating greater speed differences between you and cars traveling the speed limit, and having less time to react to a hazard. Speed also increases the probability that you will be injured or killed in a crash. This is really just a matter of F = MA. In this case, forces increase significantly with speed (that is, acceleration). At some point, the forces can overwhelm even the most crashworthy of cars. Crash types also change with speeding, including an increase in road-departure crashes that lead to rollovers and collisions with fixed objects, such as oak trees.

As with almost all risk-related contributing factors, *males are more likely than females* to be involved in a fatal speeding-related crash. (In chapter 5, I talk more about testosterone as it relates to driving.) Younger drivers speed more than older drivers, with the speeding-related fatal crash rate *almost twice as high* for drivers under the age of 34.

Extreme speeding is certainly one of the most dangerous behaviors a driver can undertake. The risk here increases exponentially because of all the factors described above *plus* the increased potential to experience a severe impact with either a moving or fixed object. Take the following scenario, for example: **if you are speeding more than 30 mph over the speed limit, your odds of being injured in a crash are between *30 and 50 times higher* (odds = 30.0–50.0) than if you are traveling within 10 mph of the speed limit.**

Pay attention to the speed of those around you. Rather than be the fastest driver, learn to go with the flow.

In terms of speed selection, you want to be traveling close to the speed limit or the speed of traffic around you. If you are slightly over the speed limit, chances are you will be in sync with traffic for the most part and will have to pass and get passed the least, meaning you can avoid more possible conflicts.

One thing I learned a long time ago is that there are many instances when you don't want to be number one. This is true at a party, where it's better to be the guy or gal who has had the second or third most to drink rather than the person who has had the most to drink. These "number ones" are often the talk of the party, though not necessarily in a good way, and they are often in trouble with their significant others. The same analogy applies to speed selection. Pay enough attention to make sure you are not the fastest driver around. If you are the fastest, you are not only at the highest risk of a serious crash, you are also likely to get a ticket sooner or later.

The moral of the story is to go with the flow!

Don't Drive Too Fast—or Too Slow

Your primary goal as a driver is to avoid conflicts with other vehicles. If you don't have any conflicts—meaning, you don't occupy the same space at the same time as other vehicles—you will never hit anyone else. The probability of a conflict increases under a variety of circumstances, including at intersections, where your path literally crosses the paths of other drivers; while changing lanes; and when there is a speed differential. As mentioned previously, both your crash risk and the resulting severity of the crash increase substantially when you speed. However, there is also greater risk of a crash if you travel at a significantly slower speed than other drivers. During both instances, you are creating what we call the speed differential, which results in a greater chance of a severe crash.

Think of your crash risk due to speed differentials as a U-shaped curve. The peaks of that curve—or your significant increased risk of an injury or fatality—represent the speed differential created by either driving much too fast or much too slow. Essentially, you do not want to deviate more than 10 mph from the speed at which the rest of traffic is traveling, or your risk will increase ... a lot.

This brings up an important point: If you can't maintain a reasonable speed for any reason—say, you lost the number three cylinder in your VW bus or you ran out of gas—get the car off of the road. If you can't get the car off the road, get out of the car, get safely onto the shoulder, run in the direction from which you were traveling in your vehicle (while well on the shoulder!), and wave your arms to warn other drivers. Really. You will look much less foolish than you would if someone hits your car at a speed differential of 60 mph.

A few winters ago, I was traveling with my friend and colleague Andy Petersen (whom I mention in the preface) when we came upon a curved bridge where we saw a car lying on its side in the right lane. A woman was in this car, sticking her head up through the driver's side window, waving for help. Turns out that the bridge had iced over before the rest of the road, and she spun out and somehow hit the guardrail and rolled over. I wondered what I should do. It was a terrible situation because traffic was still moving fast, sight distance was limited due to the curve, and the bridge was slick. The chances were very high that someone could hit her at a high speed, and she was certainly in no position to be protected from such a crash. So, having limited options in a generally unsafe situation, I slowed down, stopped, and then backed my truck down the shoulder to a straight stretch with good sight distance and traction. I parked so that my truck straddled the right lane and the shoulder. Again, this wasn't the safest option, but I thought it would work to get other drivers to both slow down and change lanes. I turned on my hazards and put out a triangle reflector. Then, I got out of the truck and went to help Andy get the woman out of her car and safely off the roadway.

Luckily, and despite the fact that I had created a hazard myself, cars slowed, and traffic eventually backed up before encountering the crashed vehicle. There is no way I would have stayed in my truck and done nothing, because getting that woman out of the car was of paramount importance due to the speed differential she was facing and the fact that the crash site could have caused an unexpected event for other drivers. I also would have been at risk by staying in my stopped truck.

Eliminate Blind Spots

Many cars these days are designed to eliminate virtually all blind spots—but only *if* you adjust your mirrors appropriately. There are several important points to consider when adjusting your mirrors:

Use all features of your mirrors to avoid blind spots. This 2016 Ford Focus has a Blind Spot Indicator.

1. **You don't need to see the side of your car.** Many people adjust their side view mirrors so that much of their car is in view. What you want to do instead is adjust your mirrors out to the point where you can *just barely* see the side of your car.

2. **Use all features of your mirrors.** In my family two of our cars have the small round convex mirrors attached to the main mirror to help eliminate blind spots. These supplementary mirrors help, but it takes a little effort and practice to make sure you are using them and not just looking at the main mirror. There are other types of mirrors, including some European models that feature a regular mirror toward the inside and a convex mirror toward the outside. The same rules apply, though: focus on using what is there. (If you have a backup camera as part of a warning system in your car, I talk more about this in chapter 11.)

3. **Checking your blind spot is still a good idea.** I have convinced myself that my car has no blind spot, but I check it anyway. Why, you ask? Because I don't completely trust that there isn't a blind spot for every kind of motorcycle, scooter, or small car on the road. And, hey, there is nothing wrong with double-checking!

4. **Make sure the mirrors aren't creating blind spots!** I have seen cases in which the mirrors themselves create blind spots to the left and right. This is particularly true of, say, a large truck or van with very tall mirrors. Sometimes, the combination of the mirror and the vehicle pillar

can hide bicycles, pedestrians, and even scooters or motorcycles. If you drive such a vehicle, it may be important to lean forward at intersections or to check three times to make sure nothing is hiding.

Be Prepared for the Snowpocalypse or Any Other Great Catastrophe ... It Could Happen to You!

I used to live in the mountains of Colorado with my first wife, Joellen. I was commuting up and down Highway 285, which was often a fascinating drive that fluctuated between 5,280 and 9,000 feet in elevation. One Friday night, Joellen and I went with some friends to a laser light show in Denver (Google it, kids). We were heading up a massive hill on Highway 285 in a rainstorm in my '71 VW bus. As often happened as we increased in elevation, the rain turned to freezing rain, and the highway became a sheet of ice. However, being a daily commuter up this road and being well-seasoned following the rollover in my '73 VW bus, I was prepared for these conditions.

We had chains, sleeping bags, a catalytic heater stashed in a storage area under a seat (because we had learned to securely stow all heavy, loose objects), pack boots, down coats, etc. As we continued our trek up the hill, we could tell that there were many nonexperienced commuters heading into the mountains for the weekend. Consequently, we soon found ourselves in a surreal landscape. Vehicles were stuck everywhere in both lanes and on both shoulders. No one was going anywhere soon because there was no way for plows or salt trucks to get through the scene. So, with nothing better to do, we got out of the bus and walked around on foot to survey the damage and assist as needed.

Soon I encountered an ill-prepared, frantic woman in a mink stole and high heels who asked for my help. I know she was frantic because she said, "Help me, I'm frantic!" I explained to her that she may as well relax for a while; she had plenty of gas to run the heat in her Thunderbird and a new enough car that she wouldn't experience fume problems.

A few cars ahead, I helped a local sheriff put on his chains because he had no gloves. As I continued to walk, I heard a car ahead really gunning the engine. As I got closer, I could tell that the driver, a man, had put chains on his tires and had apparently forged a path forward. He was trying to get out, and with

Road conditions in the Colorado mountains can vary dramatically in the winter due to extreme elevation changes. I took this photo when I lived in Colorado.

great enthusiasm, but because the road was so icy, he was just spinning in place. And then, at some point during this spectacle, part of one of the chains came loose and ruptured the gas tank. Sparks from the spinning chains ignited the gas, the tank, and soon, the whole car. Fortunately, the driver and his passenger escaped, but the car was engulfed in flames 15 or 20 feet high. There was nothing anyone could do other than watch in amazement. Joellen and I sat there on the Jersey barrier and watched for about an hour until the car had basically burned itself out. At that point, the local fire department managed to close the downhill side of the highway and get a pumper truck down the icy hill to deal with the fire. The fire department then proceeded to pump hundreds of gallons of water on the fire to make sure it was completely out. Of course, the water they pumped out only turned to more ice. Nearly six hours later the road was opened again, and we made it the rest of the way home.

The point here is to carry what you might need (properly stowed and secured in the vehicle to avoid a projectile situation!) should the unexpected happen: chains (in areas prone to inclement winter weather), flares, flashlights, reflective triangles, etc. Have a good spare tire and basic tools because even these days you may have limited cell coverage during a trip. You can buy cool little kits at any auto parts store at a minimal cost. I have friends who also stash some cash—a few hundred dollars will usually do—in their cars when taking a trip, just in case. It's much better to have it and not need it than to need it and not have it!

Another "expect the unexpected" story comes by way of my friend and colleague Zac Doerzaph. During one relatively Indian summer–like day in late November, Zac flew to Detroit from our home in southwest Virginia on a business trip. He had a light jacket and a normal suitcase full of business casual clothes appropriate for the weather. A few days later, Zac headed back home, making the return trip in a car since he was taking a last-minute opportunity to shuttle back one of our test vehicles.

Well, Zac ran into an unexpected blizzard that dumped about 18 inches of snow within a few hours, crippling the West Virginia turnpike on which he was traveling. The vehicle he was driving was not made for heavy snow, and he lacked any emergency supplies. The car wasn't his, and he had not expected to drive back home, much less spend the next 12 hours with numerous stranded motorists while authorities—including the National Guard—worked diligently to open the roadway one vehicle at a time. He had nothing with him, except slacks and polo shirts. He had no cell phone charger, very bad reception, and limited food since he gave most of what he had to a nearby mother for her toddler, and he was nearly out of gas. To deal with plummeting temperatures and to do his best to stay warm throughout the night, Zac put on both pairs of pants he had, made a turban out of his polo shirts, and curled into a ball on the floorboards and away from the cold glass of the vehicle. He got invited into the cab of a semi to warm up, but declined the kind offer ... at least, he figured, until he was desperate. Zac spent a very uncomfortable eight-hour night trying to stay warm and carefully conserve what little gas remained in the tank in the hopes that a plow might clear the way.

The point is simple. Be prepared.

3. Defensive Driving 101

Don't Hit Anything

The goal of defensive driving is to get you to your destination safely, having successfully anticipated hazards and avoided conflicts with other vehicles or objects on the road. When it comes to driving, the best defense is not a good offense, even though there may be times when most of us would wish for offensive weapons in our cars. Nothing fancy, just a few James Bond/Aston Martin kinds of machine guns and smoke bombs. The funny thing is if you mention that to the hardware guys at VTTI, they actually start trying to figure out how to do it ... anyway, I digress. The point is don't confuse defensive driving with driving aggressively. NHTSA defines the occurrence of aggressive driving as "the operation of a motor vehicle in a manner that endangers or is likely to endanger persons or property." Basically, driving aggressively means you're driving like a bat out of hell with no regard for the well-being of others. (I'll talk more about aggressive driving in chapter 7.)

Below are some tips to move you *safely* from point A to point B as a defensive driver while ensuring you do not compromise the safety of your fellow transportation users. Along the way, I'll give you points on how to avoid being the aggressor.

It's All About Time and Space

As you drive your shiny metal box of unusual size and weight, it is important to stay away from all the other shiny boxes of unusual sizes and weights. The best way to do this is to increase the space—*and the time*—between you and everything else that you might possibly come into contact with. I emphasize time because it is sometimes more important than space. For example, if you were 60 feet away from a car in a parking lot while traveling 10 mph, it would take more than four seconds until you hit the car. That's relatively an eternity in terms of having enough time to avoid a crash. By contrast, you would only have a little more than half a second to avoid a crash under the same distance while traveling 70 mph on an interstate.

Of course, an easy way to increase time and space is to *not tailgate*. Following too closely obviously decreases your space and time. If we return to making our figurative cake, there are many, many crash cases each year that begin with this ingredient (following too closely) present. In the grand scheme of things, not tailgating means you will get to where you're going two seconds later. Other ways to create more space include moving to the left lane to pass a disabled vehicle on the shoulder of a highway and giving bicycles, pedestrians, and parked cars a wide berth as you pass. These practices probably seem obvious, but if you think about them in terms of giving yourself more space and time to react if something unexpected occurs, they become good defensive driving habits.

A Most Important Defense: Stay Away from Heavy Vehicles

Here is another friendly physics lesson: a long-haul truck is 40 tons of unforgiving steel running the length of a football field every three seconds. In other words—as you will read time and again throughout this book—*stay away from trucks*.

Long-haul trucks are made up of about 40 tons of steel. Keeping space and time between you and the truck will increase your odds of avoiding a crash!

The vast majority of truck drivers are professional, safe drivers. But just like all other types of drivers, *most* does not mean *all*, and even good truck drivers occasionally get in bad situations.

About 10 years ago there was a multi-truck collision on an interstate near my home. The crash happened when a truck mowed into a line of stopped traffic while traveling at about 65 mph, with no indication of the truck driver braking beforehand. The truck driver was likely drowsy or distracted, resulting in a deadly recipe. The situation subsequently created a hazard for other drivers. Crashes like this are not terribly frequent, but they are always terrible. In this case emergency workers arrived on the scene and worked for several hours to separate two Class 8 semitrucks. After working for about two hours or so, they realized for the first time that there was a minivan sandwiched between the two trucks. The minivan was about one-third of its original length; all four of its occupants were killed instantly in the crash. There is no airbag, no crumple zone, and no five-star vehicle of any weight that would have allowed that family to survive. The forces generated in such a crash were just too great.

With this in mind, here are some facts about trucks from my friend, former student, and colleague Rich Hanowski and his staff from the VTTI Center for Truck and Bus Safety:

1. Approximately 10 percent of truck drivers account for 40 percent to 50 percent of crash and near-crash risks. Your only problem is that you don't know which ones are part of the 10 percent.
2. Two out of every five truck drivers admit to dozing or nodding off at the wheel at least once in their career.
3. Even when truck drivers are awake and alert, they are doing some kind of secondary task (like talking on a cell phone, reading something, etc.) more than 25 percent of the time.
4. A texting truck driver has 23 *times* the risk of being involved in a safety-critical event compared to a driver just traveling down the road. And truckers *do* text!

The takeaway is simple: keeping space and time between you and heavy trucks will really increase your odds of avoiding a crash with one of them. And this isn't just because truck drivers make mistakes. It is because **two out** *of every three crashes* **involving a car and a truck are the fault of the car driver.**

The large-truck fatality rate per 100 million vehicle miles traveled is 1.46, while the fatality rate for cars is 1.12 per 100 million vehicle miles traveled. So many of us can do better around truck drivers. The following tips may be of help when steering clear of trucks:

1. If you are following a truck, stay back until you are ready to pass.
2. If there is a vehicle ahead of you passing a truck, wait until that vehicle completes the pass before starting your pass. Do *not* ride alongside the truck.
3. When you are passing on either side of a truck, be wary of its blind spots. Those danger zones differ from those of cars and are located anywhere behind the truck and alongside the cab, particularly just in front of the cab on the right. Our friends at the Federal Motor Carrier Safety Administration (FMCSA) have good information about the "No Zone" of a truck. Some truck carriers also display a placard on the back of trucks indicating blind spots. The bottom line is to stay away from these areas while you drive!
4. Always pass trucks briskly, even if you have to speed up a little to pass safely. When you do make your pass, do so quickly. You do not want to linger in the blind spots of a truck for any length of time. Just keep a copy of this book in your vehicle and show it to the cops if you get pulled over for speeding up to pass a truck; tell them a safety professional told you to do it.
5. Trucks can't stop as fast as you can, so don't cut them off. Don't pass and then slow down; give truck drivers plenty of room on your briskly executed lane change.

Expect the Unexpected

Periodically, I am asked to serve as an expert witness in a legal case involving a crash. At least once per year, I get a call from an attorney representing a client—on either side of the case—involved in a crash in which a car or truck slammed into a line of vehicles with no signs of braking or slowing. Usually, the defendant was driving on the interstate and hit a plaintiff in a stalled car, truck, hay wagon, etc. More often than not, the crash occurred during ideal driving conditions: dry, clear, during the day, with a long sight distance. These crashes left behind no, or very short, skid marks before the vehicles hit.

You may ask, How could this be? How can you miss a stopped vehicle in broad daylight? That's typically what the courts ask as well. The driver must have been looking down at something or must have been falling asleep at the wheel, right? The answer is yes. Most of the time the driver was looking somewhere else, even if it was just a random glance away from the roadway. However, regardless of whether the offending driver was distracted or fatigued, in the majority of these scenarios the stopped vehicle violated the expectations of the driver. Essentially, the stopped vehicle created a key ingredient to make our figurative cake, resulting in a crash. No one *expects* a vehicle to be stopped in the left lane of an interstate, at least not on a rural interstate. It is a very rare event. And humans are notoriously bad at being alert and ready to respond to a rare event (a fact I will discuss at length later in this book). Just to give you an idea of what I'm talking about here, several of my colleagues were recently discussing some research being done with truck-mounted attenuators (TMAs), like the one pictured here.

Despite being brightly colored, work vehicles like this truck-mounted attenuator can surprise drivers if they are not alert and prepared to respond to the unexpected.

Pretty conspicuous, right? Lots of bright, flashing yellow lights ... who could possibly hit that? Well, in northern Virginia alone more than 70 TMAs were hit in 2017. Why? Because they are a great example of violating driver expectations: they are generally slow-moving or stopped altogether in work zones, where traffic would otherwise be flowing normally.

Work zones can create slowdowns and unexpected braking. Pay extra attention!

I have two pieces of advice here:

1. **Work on anticipating road hazards.** The hazard could be a service van blocking the sight distance to an intersection, or it could be a "Work Zone Ahead" or "Mowing" sign on the interstate that may create unstable traffic and a sudden slowdown. The blue lights of a police car almost always make someone hit the brakes to avoid a ticket, even if traffic is flowing only slightly above the speed limit. The hazard could be an oncoming car that is fully or partially blocked from your vision by cars in the turn lane opposite to you. You may encounter a crowded street full of pedestrians in a college town after a football game. There are just too many cases to name. The point is to work on being alert and wary when the situation demands it. Don't make assumptions about what you can't see and what other road users might do.
2. **Keep your eyes on the road.** Stay engaged in the driving task so that you

can brake hard and fast at any moment if needed. This is a hard piece of advice to follow, and I will talk about this point throughout the book. In general, though, *keep your eyes on the forward roadway*. Be aware that you have a primary task (driving) to which you must pay attention by scanning the environment, controlling your vehicle, and being ready to avoid hazards.

Don't Violate the Expectations of Other Drivers

The flip side to expecting the unexpected is to avoid being the cause of the unexpected. You will read this several times throughout this book, but you don't want other drivers to hit *you* because you violated their expectations—that is, you do not want to be the key ingredient that results in the figurative cake being made. To avoid being the unexpected, go the speed other drivers pretty much expect; get your car off the road if you have to stop; and if you can't get your car off the road, get out of the car, get to a safe place, and warn other drivers. When parking on the side of the street, check your mirrors before opening your car door. And, of course, follow the rules of the road because that's what people expect.

I was telling my friend and colleague John about this book. In addition to giving me a lot of good publishing advice, John shared one of his stories that illustrates a point about violating the expectations of other drivers. When John first began to drive, he missed an exit on the highway. Being young and inexperienced, he decided it was a good idea to back his car up on the interstate and then take the exit. No other cars were around when he started this process, but soon there was a car approaching and it hit John's car from behind. Fortunately, the driver was able to brake to the point where no one was hurt and the damage was relatively minor. I say fortunately because the truth is that road scenarios can change quickly when cars are essentially traveling the length of a football field every three seconds.

John, of course, thought that he was in serious trouble, that he would lose his newly received license for reckless driving. A police officer arrived on the scene, got both licenses, and proceeded to interview the other driver. The officer then came to John's car and said, "Here is the police report so you can make an insurance claim. That guy had some crazy story about you backing up on the interstate, but I didn't believe him and gave him a ticket. You are free to go." John learned an important lesson that day about violating the expectations of other drivers, not to mention a lesson learned about luck!

Is There a Best Way to Crash?

One of my favorite musicians is an artist named Todd Snider. (Todd, you may remember me; I was the guy with the gray beard singing out of key in the front row.) Todd wrote a very touching song called "45 Miles" about the brief moment of time between realizing you are going to wreck your car and wrecking your car. As he explains in the preamble to the song, it only has one chord because he was "pressed for time." (As of the writing of this second edition, I am proud to say that my daughter, Emily, who works in the music industry, has obtained a copy of this book signed by Todd himself. Thank you, Emily, and thank you, Todd.)

Many of us have experienced exactly what Todd is talking about. On rare occasions (made rarer still if you continue reading this book), a situation is simply not salvageable and you have no option but to hit *something*.

In such situations it is important, first and foremost, to understand what drivers typically do in the same situations so that you can increase your chances of reacting well in what is a very short time period. I performed a study with my friend, colleague, and former student Jon Hankey in which we looked at driver behavior during looming crash situations. The study was performed with several of our colleagues from NHTSA; it was Jon's dissertation when we were at the University of Iowa. Jon used a high-fidelity driving simulator for this study, creating scenarios in which drivers had to react to different cases in which a vehicle pulled out in front of them at an intersection.

A very interesting finding from this study was that drivers, when they have the least amount of time to react to an impending crash, *react the slowest*. They are also just as likely to steer as they are to brake. Why might this be the case? We believe it is because the drivers in our study saw no obvious way to avoid a crash in the split second they had to decide what to do. Without an obvious ideal choice, they took longer to consider their options. This is probably also why roughly half of them began to brake first, while half of them steered first.

Another, probably less surprising, finding from the study was that drivers steered their vehicles away from the direction in which the other vehicle was entering the roadway. For example, if the other vehicle was coming from the right, the drivers tended to steer left into the opposing lane of traffic. As I will discuss later, braking like hell and avoiding head-on collisions are really better strategies in virtually all circumstances like this.

Here's another example to illustrate what drivers often do when they are faced with the inevitable. I helped perform a study in the mid-1990s led by my friend, colleague, and former student Mike Mollenhauer that looked at driver emergency response on icy roads. This was a very cool study, literally and figuratively. We took drivers to the spillway of a dam in Iowa in January after having the local fire department spray the area with water. We told the volunteer drivers that we were trying to determine how they liked a new kind of car on slick roads (deception, which is sometimes carefully done in our line of work, but not lying). After they drove around for a while on a course we laid out, we then slid a large object that looked very heavy and ominous (it wasn't) into their path, giving them little time to react. Of course, we made sure that the drivers were in no danger, but they didn't really know what it was they were going to hit and what damage might be done to the car.

The impetus for this study was the advent of anti-lock brake systems (ABS)—a fascinating phenomenon in transportation history. After the introduction of ABS, rear-end crashes decreased slightly, but road-departure crashes increased slightly despite all expectations to the contrary. Before the creation of ABS, drivers would often try to steer but would still hit the car or object in the road because the vehicle was still skidding or sliding after the driver slammed on the brakes. Steering in a crash scenario without ABS more or less just gave the driver a false sense of security that he or she had some ounce of control. With ABS, however, drivers now had full steering control. If they steered to the right, lo and behold, they often went off the road. Why does this matter? Generally speaking, if you leave the roadway instead of hitting the car or object in front of you, you are more likely to be injured or killed because of a rollover or a collision with a fixed object, such as an oak tree.

We discovered two important points in this study. First, drivers usually steer to the right to avoid an object in front of them after slamming on the brakes. This occurs when drivers realize they don't have enough time and space to stop. As mentioned, steering to the right with ABS usually resulted in drivers going off the road. Second, most folks back then didn't know how to use ABS, despite the best efforts of car dealers everywhere to educate buyers about the system. At the very least, the drivers in this particular study reverted back to the automatic behavior of "pumping the brakes" on ice, a maneuver we were all taught in the dark ages. However, the correct response in an ABS-equipped car is to squeeze the brakes hard until they "chatter." If you have never experienced the chattering sound of ABS brakes, it can be a bit disconcerting, but it is a very good sign. The chatter should reassure you that your car is pumping the brakes for you at a much faster rate and more effectively than you can move your foot. Essentially, a modern car and a driver who knows how the car works make a great pair when it comes to avoiding crashes.

There are several other considerations that should guide our brief thoughts when faced with an imminent crash: fixed objects, delta-V, and vulnerable road users.

My friend Gene Farber, who passed away a number of years ago and is mentioned in more detail later in this book, used to tell a story about his days working at Ford. Gene had the opportunity to actually sit in a car during a low-speed crash test. The test was designed to run a car into a solid wall at 10 mph. Gene thought what most of us would think: "How bad could it be? It's only 10 mph." It ended up being a shocking and bone-jarring experience for Gene, and he was physically sore for several days. Now, imagine what hitting an oak tree at 60 mph would feel like.

When it comes to hitting a solid, fixed object, a rule of thumb is that the potential for injury is the same as hitting a moving object at twice the speed you are traveling. Cars are considered "moving" objects even when they are stopped because they move and deform (bend, crumple, etc.) when you hit them. This rule breaks down to some extent for head-on collisions because the moving object is about to exert tremendous force on you as part of the equation. This brings us to delta-V, which is also known as change in velocity, or the total speed between two colliding objects. If you are traveling at, say, 60 mph, a head-on collision has a delta-V of 120 mph if we assume the other car is also traveling at 60 mph. If you hit a stationary car while traveling at 60 mph, the delta-V is just your speed.

Now let's consider crashes involving vulnerable road users—pedestrians, cyclists, folks on scooters or mopeds, or motorcyclists. If there is any way to avoid hitting a vulnerable road user, you should do so. If you think back to the F = MA equation, you are on the side with a higher mass, meaning you are going to exert a whole lot of force with your vehicle. On top of that, these folks have very little protection against metal traveling at high rates of speed, so the outcome is often fatal for them.

Killing someone, regardless of the circumstances, will change your life in a bad way on so many levels, not to mention the devastation you'll cause for everyone involved. Be alert, attentive, and courteous around vulnerable road users. Even if you have to wait 20 seconds to safely pass a bicyclist, that cyclist's life is worth more than your time.

The reason I am telling you all this is to give you a strategy for what to hit if you have limited choices and you know you are going to crash. I have seen alert, attentive, and sober drivers do some amazing things to avoid crashes, a fact I will later discuss in greater detail. However, if you are "pressed for time" in a crash scenario and can't really carefully consider your options, here are a few very simple rules that may help you:

1. **Don't steer left, thereby risking a head-on collision.** Due to its significant delta-V, a head-on collision has the highest injury and fatality rates of any crash type. **The rate of fatality in a head-on collision is *three times higher* than a road-departure crash and 41 *times higher* than a rear-end crash.** This is why you may have heard the phrase "take the ditch" in the context of dealing with someone crossing the center line heading toward you. Life is more complicated than that, however, and there are always exceptions. For instance, if you are in the left lane of a divided highway and have the choice between slamming into a line of stopped traffic at 60 mph (maybe because you were tired or distracted or you were just not expecting stopped traffic) or steering left into the median, the median may be a good choice.

2. **Avoid the ditch if you can at all help it.** Although better than a head-on crash, road departure crashes are also very bad. **The rate of fatality or injury in a road-departure crash is *roughly 14 times higher* than a rear-end crash.** Steering into a ditch may put you in the path of fixed objects or could lead to a rollover. As described earlier, you may have a

natural tendency to steer right. If so, try to keep your vehicle on the shoulder if there is one and you can perform such a maneuver.

Before the advent of anti-lock braking systems (ABS), drivers were taught to "pump the brakes" on ice and snow, but the correct response in ABS-equipped cars is to squeeze the brakes hard until they "chatter."

3. **Brake like hell!** A fascinating aspect of driver behavior is that most drivers brake at only about 60 percent of the vehicle's braking ability before a rear-end crash. Braking to a car's limit is something we rarely do. Most often, we are worried about upsetting passengers or spilling coffee. Take the family out to the local shopping mall with no one around and *slam on the brakes!* Have everyone try it a few times. That way, you will be ready when you are about to crash and can hit the brakes hard and fast with absolutely no hesitation. Believe me when I tell you that it's easier to apologize to your spouse after a hard brake than after a crash, and getting coffee stains out of your carpet at an auto detailer is cheaper than any trip to a body shop. Again, there are some exceptions. If you brake to the limit of your car's ability, you should pat yourself on the back for that brief moment ... until the driver

behind you hits you because he or she is only braking at 60 percent capacity. Remember, if someone is behind you when you brake hard to avoid a crash, you become the one violating expectations in such a scenario. But hey, at least you won't get a ticket, and your insurance rates won't go up. Two words of advice here: keep an extra copy of this book in your car to give to the person who just hit you so they will know to brake harder, and be alert and attentive so you can generally avoid having to brake hard and get hit from behind.

4. ***Buy a car that brakes like hell!*** VTTI completed an analysis of key crash risk factors using the Second Strategic Highway Research Program Naturalistic Driving Study. This is the largest naturalistic study of its kind to date, involving more than 3,500 drivers from six data collection sites across the US, with nearly 2,000 crashes identified from among those drivers. In our analysis, we looked at 905 of the crashes that were higher in severity, meaning they involved injuries and/or property damage, and found that **nearly 70 percent of crashes involved the driver engaging in some type of observable distraction.** Those of us at VTTI have believed that for some time this key "cake" ingredient has been present in large quantities of crashes based on our study trends. However, this analysis marks the first time such data have been substantiated using the largest crash-only data set available for light vehicles. Meanwhile, NHTSA is adding to its star-rating system automatic emergency braking (AEB), such as crash-imminent braking (meaning, the car brakes automatically if it believes you are about to crash) and dynamic brake support (that is, the car senses that you hit the brakes hard and automatically takes you from the 60 percent capacity level to the maximum braking level the car can perform). These systems may help greatly with the US crash problem, but only time will tell. NHTSA does not require AEB on all new cars, though it can choose to mandate such. However, even without a NHTSA requirement, four auto manufacturers voluntarily made it standard in more than one-half of their 2017 vehicles, and another five made it standard in about 30 percent of their 2017 vehicles; 20 have volunteered to equip their new passenger vehicles with AEB by 2022.

Hit Bambi, Thumper, and Rocky If You Have to ... But Maybe not Bullwinkle

Pop quiz: What is the most dangerous animal in the United States?

1. Venomous snakes
2. Sharks
3. Black widow and brown recluse spiders
4. Deer

The answer is deer, by a large margin. State Farm estimates that each year more than 1.3 million crashes in the US are caused by the presence of deer. By contrast, about six people die in the US from wild venomous snake bites per year (which does not include another six or so who die from "snake handling" or religious ceremonies); about seven die from spider bites. On average, shark attacks cause one fatality every two years in the United States.

More than 1.3 million crashes in the US involve deer.

Senator John Warner of Virginia (now retired) helped VTTI become the National Surface Transportation Safety Center for Excellence, which was a congressional designation. When the building that housed the center was dedicated, Senator Warner was in attendance. During the dedication luncheon, he told me that he often sees deer while driving around Virginia and asked whether he should just hit the deer or veer into the ditch when faced with a crash situation.

Being the researcher that I am and full of facts, I explained that the odds were dependent on the type of vehicle he was driving. Semitruck drivers should always hit the deer, I explained, as well as SUV drivers. However, if you are driving a two-seater convertible, it depends.

The senator, slightly less patiently, asked simply, "Do I hit the deer or not?" Again, I began to explain the factors at play in such a situation, to which he replied, "You aren't answering my question." As I began again, Gary Allen, a friend and colleague from the Virginia Department of Transportation, said, "Hit the deer, Senator." That response satisfied the senator greatly, and he then went on to tell a fascinating story about when he was married to Elizabeth Taylor (a story for a different book, I suppose).

There I am with Senator John Warner (left).

The point here is very similar to the point made earlier about *how* to crash when it is inevitable. While some deaths occur from a large animal coming through the windshield, most deaths occur when drivers depart the road to avoid hitting the animal.

That is, the odds are in your favor if you stay on the road, in your lane, and hit the animal rather than veering off the road to avoid it. This is certainly true of opossums, skunks, squirrels, and even dogs and cats, although somewhat less so with moose. Now, this doesn't mean you shouldn't *brake like hell* as I described previously. However, even when braking rapidly and as hard as you can, you should be at least a little wary of a secondary crash occurring if you are in traffic. Overall, though, stay in your lane unless you see a much better option like safely steering to a shoulder.

Stay Alert and Be Wary!

As described in the preface to this book, VTTI has conducted many naturalistic driving studies that require putting tiny cameras, radar, and other sensors in people's own cars while they go about their everyday lives. We have data from enough cars, trucks, and motorcycles (about 4,000) over enough time (studies have lasted up to three years) to capture a lot of crashes (nearly 2,000 and counting).

Having watched many crashes in the resulting naturalistic driving videos, one thing I can tell you is that the most common crash occurrence has at least two key ingredients present to make our figurative cake: (1) the driver is not looking at the road, and (2) something unexpected happens in front of the driver's car. There are often other elements at play, but these two factors combined are very common in a crash. I will talk at some length about the risks of taking your eyes off of the road, but I wanted to bring it up here in the context of defensive driving. So, here are a few tips to help you avoid crashes:

1. **You need to be able to see far enough ahead.** This is the concept of sight distance—that is, the distance in terms of both space and time that you can see when you look. And sight distance changes all the time due to traffic, weather, curves and hills, vegetation, etc. Get used to paying attention to not only how far you can see but how fast things might change. I'll give you an example of an intersection near where I used to live. When I stopped at the stop sign, I needed to make a left-hand turn, but the sight distance to the right was very short, the speeds were relatively high (about 45 mph), and there were often trucks headed to the local rock quarry. I literally had to make sure there was no traffic to the left and stare to the right as I pulled out, prepared to hit the gas if

needed. If I did a normal right-left, right-left look as they teach you in driver's ed class, I would have been mowed over a time or two by a 10-wheeled dump truck.

2. **Look far down the road and plan ahead.** Relative to sight distance, use whatever you have. If you can see far ahead, look far ahead. As with most everything in life, there is an exception to this rule: you need to be wary of closer objects like parked cars, pedestrians, and so on, particularly if you are traveling in an urban area. However, you still want to shift your gaze to look ahead in this environment to the extent feasible. Look ahead and through the windows and windshields of other vehicles for brake lights. This strategy allows you to make maneuvers such as braking or changing lanes without any sudden moves, thus helping you avoid conflicts with other vehicles. It also helps you avoid getting trapped behind cars on the highway.

3. **Look and see.** If you look at crash databases, there is a factor in some crashes called "looked but failed to see." This factor is thought to be a key "cake" ingredient in roughly 10 percent of crashes. In these cases, the driver typically states that he or she looked in the direction necessary but didn't see the other vehicle or whatever else was coming. This may be because the driver went through the motions to look but wasn't really processing the information because he or she was thinking about something else, the driver's view was at least partially blocked by the structure of the car (maybe a blind spot), the object the driver hit wasn't very conspicuous (perhaps a bicycle rider in gray clothing traveling against a grayish background), and/or the driver was looking for something specific. You would be surprised at the number of cases in which a crash occurs because a driver was looking for a car and instead overlooked a truck, pulling out in front of the truck and hitting it. In any event, it is important to focus on looking hard and looking long enough to see anything that may be "hiding."

4. **Look out for the looming threshold.** Brake lights ahead convey the simple message that the driver has his or her foot on the brake. Most of the time, the driver is just resting his or her foot on the brake and is getting ready to slow or is slowing gently. However, once in a while, the driver ahead is slamming on the brakes. Unfortunately, the brake lights look the same regardless of the level of braking. If you are pretty close to the car, you may get other cues that the driver has slammed on the brakes. Notably, as you rapidly approach the stopping car, the visual angle (or

the size of the car in your visual field) gets larger pretty quickly. This is called *looming*. At some distance away, you don't notice this looming because you are outside of what is called the *looming threshold*, where the size of the car in your visual field does not change very fast. In such cases of being outside the looming threshold, you really can't tell the difference between a gentle brake and a hard brake maneuver. I have seen a number of crash cases during which Driver One looked away for a second or two when brake lights came on ahead, having assumed that Driver Two was applying a gentle brake. However, in these cases, Driver Two had slammed on his or her brakes; by the time Driver One looked back at the road, there was no time to stop. Remember that if brake lights come on, keep looking until you know what the situation is and can react accordingly.

Brake lights on the cars ahead let you know that drivers are braking. However, if you are outside the "looming threshold," you may not be able to react quickly enough to avoid a crash.

Watch Out for Impaired Drivers!

I am using *impaired* in the broadest sense for this discussion, including being drowsy, distracted, drunk, and/or drugged. Not too many years ago, when you saw a car weaving out of the lane, chances were pretty good that you were witnessing a drunk driver. Now, you might be witnessing a driver texting, a driver checking stock on his or her smartphone, or a driver falling asleep at the wheel. The symptoms are mostly the same, but they should tell you the following: be aware of who is doing what, be wary, and stay away! The most obvious indicator of an impaired driver is an inability to keep his or her vehicle in the travel lane. Beyond that, you should look for signs of the degree of impairment. If the offending driver is weaving a little out of the lane to the right onto an open shoulder, it could just be a momentary distraction and the driver is otherwise sober. If the offending driver is weaving in both directions and appears to be overcorrecting, or if the driver is weaving more than a couple of feet out of the lane, or if you see such behavior exhibited two or more times during the span of just a few minutes, then you are driving near a hazard. You need to go out of your way to avoid this hazard.

Other less obvious impaired behaviors include an inability to maintain speed. Drivers who continually speed up and slow down are typically impaired in some form. Also, watch out for inappropriate speeds that include drivers traveling too fast or too slow beyond what is reasonable.

Avoiding impaired drivers is a tip that can save your life. If you don't believe me, I will give you a statistic that should scare the hell out of you: **more than 13 percent of drivers involved in fatal crashes** have invalid licenses or no license at all. In the good ol' US of A it's not easy to get your license revoked. Far and away, the easiest and most common way to lose your license is to get a DUI. However, engaging in other reckless behaviors, such as getting a second or third reckless driving conviction, will get you there as well. In any event, you should always watch other drivers and be wary.

4. Adapt, Overcome, and Survive

As drivers we frequently adapt to the conditions around us. Sometimes we do so consciously, sometimes unconsciously. For example, most of us instinctively know that driving in city traffic is different than driving on an interstate or on rural roadways. The conditions are different, and we understand that we need to adapt accordingly.

The unfortunate part is that while we as drivers are accustomed to adapting, we are not always good at judging risk. Take, for instance, driving in bad weather. Those of us accustomed to driving in snow and ice know that we need to slow down during a winter storm to avoid losing control of our cars. Drivers in the South, however, don't always understand this in the same way because they don't have as much experience driving in icy conditions. They are unfamiliar with the risk and therefore can't judge it accurately. This is what happened in Atlanta in January 2014, when enough drivers failed to adapt to icy conditions and crashed, closing major roadways for several days.

What makes all of this especially dangerous is the simple fact that no matter how good you may be at adapting to your driving conditions, you are sharing the road with other drivers whom you have no control over. Chances are that some of these drivers will not be as good as you are at adapting and some will not be as good at judging their risks. Consider this statistic: VTTI studies have shown that **roughly 10 percent of drivers create between 40 and 50 percent of the overall crash risk**.

A big part of this statistic is that the drivers who make up this 10 percent don't know how, or choose not, to adapt. It's a mind-boggling fact, but it's true. Therefore, it's important that you and your family, kids, friends, and dogs not only avoid being among the 10 percent but also know how to watch out for those 10 percent!

VTTI conducts naturalistic driving studies that provide plenty of examples to illustrate this point. We see drivers who never have a near crash, a term I'll use throughout this book that essentially means having a close call. By contrast, we see drivers who experience dozens of near crashes and a few crashes or minor collisions. Not surprisingly, these latter drivers are usually distracted, at times by some pretty remarkable acts, such as removing a tongue stud while simultaneously talking on a handheld phone and driving 70 mph (for those of you who may not know, it takes both hands to remove a tongue stud). Or driving while eating … with chopsticks. Or having a passenger hold the wheel while lighting a two-foot bong. These drivers are part of the 10 percent, and it's obvious that they have issues gauging perceived and actual risks.

But lest ye have never been sitting in a ditch next to an icy road, or climbed sheepishly out of a car explaining why you didn't stop in time, or had to make up a story about the inadequacies of speed limit signs, do not cast the first stone upon your brethren. Because as you will learn, driving safety is no simple matter and we are all at risk. I have studied the subject for more than 35 years and still have much to learn, as do my numerous bright colleagues.

In truth, we all adapt when we drive. Adaptation can be both good (if you adapt to maintain a low level of risk) and bad (if you don't adapt enough or if you don't perceive the change in risk).

In the remainder of this chapter I will offer suggestions for minimizing your risk by adapting to the different conditions and scenarios you are likely to encounter.

Adaptation 101: Road and Traffic Conditions

As I've noted before, crashes are most likely to occur when an unexpected event happens while the driver is looking away from the road due to distraction, fatigue, or a desire to just look around. Often, the unexpected event is related in some way to the road the car is traveling on or the traffic conditions at that moment. Learning to adapt appropriately is key to minimizing your risk, probably as much as any other aspect of safe driving.

The Road You Are Driving on Matters

Roads are much safer than they were just 15 or 20 years ago, and they are getting better all the time. Better sight distances, wide shoulders, interchanges instead of intersections, lighting in key locations, better markings, and "roadside hardware," including different types of barriers and guardrails, have all made a real difference to road safety. Nevertheless, your level of risk varies dramatically depending on the type of road on which you are traveling. For example, **you are 2.4 *times more likely* (odds = 2.4) to get in a crash on a two-lane road than on a divided highway.**

Your risk varies by road type, so adapt accordingly

As drivers, we have the ability to reduce our risk simply by choosing interstates and divided highways over, say, back roads. Of course, we don't always have a choice when mapping out our routes, which is why I have chosen not to talk extensively about this point. What is more instructive–because we have more control over it–is our ability to *adapt* successfully to whatever kind of road you travel.

I met my wife Melissa in graduate school. We were working in the same lab, doing driving safety research with our adviser, Walt Wierwille, who was a pioneer in studying safety factors such as steering control, drowsiness, and visual attention. For Melissa's master's thesis she examined the attention required to drive on different kinds of roads, including rural curvy two-lane, straight two-lane, four-lane, and divided highways. She and I measured parameters like sight distance, road width, shoulder width, obstacle presence, posted speeds, etc. She found that different road types require different levels of attention from drivers. For example, interstates require less attention than rural roads. This was not surprising; the surprising part was *the degree to which* different roads require different levels of attention. You have to keep your eyes on a curvy roadway just to keep your car on the road. By contrast, if you're traveling on an interstate, you can take your eyes off the road for a relatively longer amount of time (which still needs to be less than two seconds–more on that later) and still keep your vehicle in your travel lane. Of course, taking your eyes off the interstate won't help you avoid hitting something in your lane. The point here is that you always need to pay attention to the type of road you are on—and then be sure to adapt accordingly.

Traffic Stability

Another important safety factor that requires drivers to adapt is traffic stability. The fact is **you are *one-half as likely* (odds = 0.5) to get in a crash when traffic is light and free-flowing compared to when roads are congested and traffic is unstable.**

The key word here is *unstable*. On the one hand, traffic can be congested to the point that all cars are moving slowly, in which case you are less likely to get injured because you (and everyone else on the road) are traveling at a lower speed. On the other hand, traffic can be congested, but not to the extent that vehicles have to slow down or stop. It's when vehicles are moving unpredictably—slowing down and speeding up—that the risk of crash rises.

Crashes are most likely to occur when an unexpected event happens while the driver is looking away from the road for any reason, including visual or manual distraction.

Unpredictability makes it harder for you to adapt because the conditions are unstable. In such cases, the best way to adapt overall is to stay focused and always keep your eyes on the road.This means resisting the temptation to eat that hamburger or to stare at those ponies in the nearby field until the road demand is low. Also, you can usually slow down, which is a good strategy as long as you're not going too slow or unexpectedly slow to the point that you impede the flow of traffic. To keep yourself safe while driving, you need to be wary and adapt more than you may think necessary.

When they were in high school, my son, Chris, and his friend Nick were taking a three-hour trip back home from a concert. They ran into heavy traffic on the highway, which slowed them down considerably. My son was taking a nap in the passenger seat while Nick was driving a shift. Being the conscientious friend that Nick was, he was listening to music on his iPod through his earbuds so that Chris could sleep. While understandable, this move also increased the risk of a typical crash ingredient: distraction.

Nick looked down momentarily at his iPod right as traffic stopped, causing Nick to hit the car in front. The unexpected had become more likely, and the key ingredients combined to make our figurative cake. No one was hurt, but the car sustained some damage. At that point, my concern turned to the fact that they were traveling in Chris's car. So, there was an insurance claim, which Nick paid for in full. No harm, no foul, except that Nick remained on my policy for a couple of years afterward, despite our efforts to explain to the insurance company that he was not a family member or primary driver of the car.

Bad Weather

According to the Federal Highway Administration (FHWA), nearly one-quarter of crashes are related to weather. Driving in bad weather (rain, snow, fog, sleet, freezing rain) increases your risk of a crash due to reduced visibility and/or reduced traction. As a rule of thumb, **bad weather increases your risk of a crash between 70 and 80 percent.**

The main reasons for the increased risk are usually visibility or traction—or both. Let's start with visibility. Almost every year, somewhere in some state there is a huge pileup on a foggy interstate. The issue in such cases is not traction but visibility. Complicating matters is the added variable of drivers encountering the unexpected. In a nutshell, drivers don't really expect to see stopped cars on the interstate, so they often don't adapt enough to that possibility, even in heavy fog. If you think about a 50- or 60-vehicle pileup, a significant number of those drivers never expected to find stopped vehicles in front of them. Consequently, they didn't adapt enough to the fact that they couldn't see.

When driving in low-visibility conditions, think about how far ahead you can see and the effect this has on your ability to stop in a timely manner.

At VTTI we have a group of test tracks collectively called the Smart Roads on which we can make fog (as well as rain and snow). We are often asked to do fog research aimed at finding ways to slow people down when they can't see. My friend and colleague Ron Gibbons conducts a lot of this visibility research for the VTTI Center for Infrastructure-Based Safety Systems. Based on that research, I have four pieces of advice if you find yourself in a low-visibility situation:

1. **Slow down.** Think about how far you can see ahead of you and the effect this has on your ability to stop in a timely manner. In order to stop in a timely manner, you don't want to drive faster than you can process the potential hazards ahead. As you will learn throughout this book, this usually means driving more slowly than you probably thought necessary in order to make a stop.
2. **Focus on the road ahead.** Actively search for any signs of cars ahead, even though it's not particularly pleasant to stare into a uniform scene of fog or snow. Don't get distracted, and don't look away from the road.
3. **If your lights are off, turn them on—in most cases on low beam.** This not only helps you see a bit better but also makes you more conspicuous to drivers behind you.
4. **Don't become a target that others can't see.** In general, this means staying out of the left lane. If you are going really slow, turn on your emergency hazards so that you are more conspicuous to those traveling behind you. If you need to stop, move over to the shoulder if you can.

The other part of the bad weather equation is traction. My first job out of college was working as a human factors engineer for a large aerospace company. I lived in the mountains of Colorado and commuted each day down the aforementioned Highway 285 to the suburbs just west of Denver. For those of you who haven't experienced living and commuting at a high altitude, concepts like "southern exposure" are very important when you live at 9,000 feet. This mostly meant that my house had snow around it until the end of May, while my neighbor across the street was enjoying bright, spring-like weather in mid-March because he faced south. It also meant that I did plenty of winter driving, which gave me ample opportunity not just to observe but to participate in bad weather conditions made worse by big uphill and downhill stretches.

One particular observation stands out from those days. Many of the commuters along Highway 285 had big pickup trucks with oversized tires and four-wheel drive. Admittedly, the knobby tires and extra drive wheels were handy in that they enabled drivers to get through some slick spots and deep snow. It's a misconception, however, that such trucks stop faster or steer better than any other car or truck traveling at highway speeds while going downhill on an icy road. If you think about it, even a two-wheel-drive car or truck has brakes on all four wheels. A newer car has anti-lock brake systems

(ABS) and maybe even electronic stability control (ESC). The point is ground clearance and four-wheel drive do not help you stop faster on ice. This is why, during my Highway 285 adventures, I often came across four-wheel-drive trucks stuck in the median, against the guardrail, or in the ditch. It was a good day when they were still "shiny side up."

Fog production on the Smart Road at VTTI.

When traction is low, you have to think a lot about momentum. Momentum is the quantity of motion of a moving object, mathematically defined as mass (weight) times speed. Momentum can be your best friend, and it can be your worst enemy. Essentially, if you are driving in a straight line on a very slick road, your vehicle will tend to keep going straight and remain at the same speed. Steering and braking are much less effective in such a scenario because the traction is so low that the tires don't grip to exert much force, even if you have a four-wheel-drive truck.

This means you have to do everything ahead of time and in slow motion during bad weather. In general, you want to control momentum by driving more slowly, particularly if the roads are icy. If you are coming to a stop sign, for example, reduced speed will help you safely maneuver to a stop in a safe place and not 20 feet into the intersection. Planning ahead will also help you. Begin to gently brake much farther in advance than you normally would to avoid skidding. If you are going downhill, reduce your speed even more and start slowing down even farther in advance because gravity is working against you, literally pulling you down the hill. The same principle applies when making a turn. Brake gently and reduce your speed well ahead of a turn. If you wait too long, you will go straight, no matter what you do with the brakes or steering wheel.

We have all heard this, but the next time it's icy, take the family to a big parking lot and practice, practice, practice all of these driving scenarios! Stop as fast as you can, feeling the beautiful chatter of your ABS and how the vehicle reacts on a slick surface; spin out and correct a slide; practice stopping at the right spot.

Of course, there's another side to the momentum equation. If you are in a vehicle that is stuck in snow or ice, you will need more momentum to get free and move forward. You want just enough momentum, but not too much! This may seem obvious, but I need to emphasize the point because it's easy to forget it when you are in the moment. For example, when you are going up a hill that is slippery, you want to start with a run-and-go at the bottom of the hill. That is, you want to build sufficient momentum to take you to the top of the hill without sliding back down. However, remember that when you reach the crest of the hill, you have to switch very quickly from generating momentum to losing momentum.

When driving in the winter, if you get stuck in a travel lane, get out of the car and get to a safe spot on the shoulder, just as you would in the case of a disabled vehicle. The tendency to want to push the car is only a good idea if you're absolutely sure you're not going to be squished by the next car that also happens to be traveling on ice!

Finally, a great way to avoid the risk associated with bad weather is to stay home—if possible. Don't get me wrong: I am *not* saying that we should all stay home when it's drizzling outside. Let's just say that when your local law enforcement and weather forecaster say to avoid travel due to inclement weather, you would be wise to heed their advice. Remember, the risk of a fatal or injurious crash is much higher during bad weather. So again, if you must drive, then you must *adapt*! Stay engaged in the driving task, keep your eyes on the road, and slow down when traction or visibility is limited.

Adaptation 102: When Your Car Is Not Your Car

Another friend and colleague, Mike Perel, worked for NHTSA for more than 40 years until he retired a few years ago. Mike participated in many, many studies during those years. One study that was particularly important to this narrative focused on the risk that comes from driving an unfamiliar car or motorcycle. Mike and NHTSA found that **if you are unfamiliar with the car you are driving, you are** *two to three times more likely* **(odds = 2.0–3.0) to get in a crash compared to driving a car with which you are familiar.**

Being unfamiliar with the car means having less than 500 miles of experience driving the vehicle. This risk applies to new cars, rental cars, and borrowed cars. However, this fact is becoming more relevant as we enter an era when ride and car sharing is becoming increasingly popular. This statistic also applies to motorcycles, which have the same or even a greater risk level.

At least two factors are at play here. First, different vehicles sometimes have significantly different handling and braking characteristics. The more differences among the vehicles, such as a compact car versus an SUV, the greater the risk when you first start driving an unfamiliar vehicle. I have seen a number of cases during which someone gets into a crash or near crash because they were driving a friend's SUV when they had pretty much only driven small cars in the past.

The second factor has to do with unfamiliar controls. You don't have to drive many different cars before you start pulling out your hair trying to figure out how to turn on the damned windshield wipers when it starts to pour rain. If you're like me, you don't even have to look past your own driveway to find several vehicles with different controls that present limitless frustration. If you add in all of the unfamiliar controls, you start to realize that you just spent the better part of a minute trying to figure out how to find your favorite classic rock or alternative station in a desperate attempt to get Justin Bieber out of your head.

The problem with unfamiliarity is almost certainly worse with motorcycles, simply because they vary in so many ways. I talk about this in a later chapter, but one motorcycle is a completely different animal from the next one. The horsepower of a Suzuki GSX-R is more than double that of a Harley Electra

Glide! Other than having (mostly) two wheels, they don't have much else in common among themselves.

In 2001 I testified before Congress on the safety implications of using cell phones and other electronic devices while driving. I am flanked by former NHTSA researchers Mike Perel (left) and Mike Goodman (right).

So ... adapt! When you are first driving an unfamiliar vehicle, take a minute or two to figure out how the most important controls work, such as lights and windshield wipers. Set the temperature before you put the car in gear so that you will be comfortable, and set up the stereo so that you are good to go before you go. Then when you do go, be overly cautious, especially when making turns and corners. Give yourself more space and time till you've had a chance to adjust to a car that is different from the one you normally drive.

Adaptation 103: When You Are Not Yourself

By now you've learned that driving is a highly dynamic activity. The roads, road conditions, traffic conditions, and even vehicles around you are constantly changing, which means that you need to change with them by reducing your speed, staying more focused, etc. The other dynamic part of the equation is *you*. Sometimes you are a better, more capable, and more engaged driver than you are at other times. One of the more surprising findings to come out of a VTTI naturalistic driving study was the tremendous impact emotions have on driver risk. I call it surprising because no other naturalistic study, to my knowledge, has found emotions to be a risk factor. However, we determined that if you are visibly emotional while driving—if you're sad, angry, crying, or agitated—your risk **increases by nearly 10 times (odds = 10.0) compared to normal driving.**

A key to avoiding crashes is understanding and acknowledging those times when you are disengaged from the primary task of driving and to modify your behavior accordingly. Here are some tips and advice on doing so:

1. If you have been drinking (within the legal limit and even well below), taking prescription medication, smoking marijuana, or have any other impairment, let someone else drive if at all possible. However, if you have no option, you need to adapt. Adapt before you drive by *not* doing whatever it is you are doing for a good, long while prior to leaving. Essentially, leave later, when you are in a more alert and sober state. During your drive, adapting means driving slower, minimizing any distractions, staying engaged while driving, and avoiding areas with heavy traffic and vulnerable road users, such as pedestrians or bicyclists.

2. If you are experiencing serious stress, your driving ability is likely to be impaired. Studies have shown that drivers under interpersonal, marital, vocational, or financial stress are *nearly four times more likely* **(odds = 4.0)** to be involved in a crash than those who are not under such stress. Big sources of stress include tragedies in your life (death of a loved one, divorce or marital separation, or serious illness) as well as other life-changing events (marriage, pregnancy, retirement, or buying a new home). It's important to be aware of these changes and understand that they may affect your driving. If you know of someone going through a tough time or a life-changing event, offer to drive them. If you are the one experiencing a stressful time, focus on staying engaged in driving, take extra time to get to your destination, stop more often during a long trip, drive slower, and leave more time and space around you. Better yet, simply remove yourself from the driving task and ask a friend or family member to drive.

3. Be prepared to adapt more as you grow older. As the overall population of the US ages over the next 25 years, the driving population will also

age. Most of us want to maintain our mobility as long as possible, but this comes with risks. A key to maintaining mobility is to adapt to your changes in capability. Fortunately, older drivers tend to do a good job of adapting for a long time. I'll discuss senior driver issues later in the book, so look for more key points in that chapter.

5. Do Not Mix Mind-Altering Substances with Driving

I often ask my transportation safety classes and other groups, "What is the most dangerous, mind-altering substance when it comes to driving?" Almost invariably, they say, "Alcohol." Sometimes I get an occasional answer of "LSD" or "shrooms" in my college classes, although I am not sure those answers come from a scientific source. Interestingly, marijuana is seldom mentioned. I will talk about this later, but in general I suspect that my students understand that it's difficult to get into a crash while sitting on the couch eating cheese puffs. However, when all factors are considered, I believe that the most dangerous mind-altering substance is testosterone.

Battle of the Sexes

Who has the most testosterone? Young males. Who are the riskiest drivers by a wide margin? Young males. Notice I said "riskiest" and not "worst." Many young males will argue fervently against this claim (largely in my opinion because they are laden with testosterone). As young males often do, they will talk about performance criteria, such as reaction time or their ability to take curves faster or their ability to drive in snow. Unfortunately, performance and skill do not matter as much in reducing crash risk as *judgment*, and young males are more prone to errors in judgment. Some of the most common judgment errors involve the following:

- Driving faster
- Driving with shorter headways (tailgating)
- Driving impaired due to alcohol
- Engaging in distracting tasks, such as texting
- Engaging in distracting tasks at the worst possible times (intersections, taking curves, etc.)

I should mention that gender makes no difference whatsoever when it comes to *driving ability*, but the same cannot be said of driver *judgment*. While young females undertake some of the same bad driving habits as males, they do so less often as a population. Still, if you are a female and you *choose* to engage in these risky behaviors, you will be at just as much risk as your male counterparts.

Dude, Where's My Car?

Driving over the legal alcohol limit is always a bad idea. Alcohol reduces inhibition, increases self-confidence and susceptibility to social influence, reduces attention, promotes secondary task engagement, and reduces reaction time. All of these traits are bad for driving, which is why **your odds of being in a fatal crash at the legal BAC limit of 0.08 percent are** *about seven times higher* **(odds = 7.0) than when you drive sober.**

For my daughter, who is 120 pounds soaking wet, that means no more than two glasses (5 oz. each) of wine in an hour. For me (a svelte 185 pounds ... or so), that means no more than four glasses of wine in an hour. At a BAC above 0.08 percent, the odds climb to very high levels. **At about twice the legal limit (0.15 percent BAC), your odds of being in a fatal crash skyrocket 300 to 600** *times higher* **(odds = 300.0–600.0) depending on your age and gender.**

Never, never, never let anyone drive a car who is in this kind of shape. A BAC of 0.15 percent essentially means doubling the above alcohol allowance numbers for my daughter and me (that is, four servings for her in an hour, and eight for me). And the younger you are, the greater the risk of a fatal crash when at an increased BAC level. If you are female, you are at greater risk of a fatal crash than your male counterparts when your BAC level increases. (This is the only time in this book that such can be said of female versus male drivers.) In most cases, the risk level is extreme, ending in the death of *the driver*. With any luck at all, you will just kill your fool self and no one else while driving under the influence. If you kill someone else, it only gets worse.

Pop quiz: Is it better to (a) take 1,000 cab, Uber, or Lyft rides home or (b) drive drunk once and end up with a DUI? They cost about the same. Think about it. For most folks, a DUI equates to a lifetime of being chauffeured around. For example, if you decide to drink heavily once per week away from home, you can take a cab home for the next 20 *years* at the same cost of one DUI. How can you tell if you need a cab? You can get a free BAC calculator app for your smartphone, or you can buy a cheap pocket Breathalyzer. You can even calculate your BAC in your head; the only complicating factors are portion size and alcohol content (think big glasses of wine or strong beers). But the moral of the story is just don't drive drunk. Period.

Your odds of being in a fatal crash at the legal blood alcohol limit of 0.08 percent are about seven times higher than driving sober. Don't risk it!

Around our small college town, we occasionally see a guy riding around on a 49.5cc motor scooter. He is the classic example of a character I refer to as "DUI-Guy." Typically, DUI-Guy is between the ages of 20 and 40. You might think this guy is environmentally conscious or is trying to save money on gas … until you pass the same guy in a rainstorm or in the winter on icy roads. Then you think, well, this guy must have been convicted of driving under the influence of alcohol, and the only way he can get around is on a scooter because it doesn't require a driver's license, license plate, or insurance. Frequently, DUI-Guys wear full-face helmets. Do you think it's because they are super safe or because they don't want anyone to know who they are? I'll let you be the judge.

The good news about DUI-Guy is that he probably didn't kill or injure someone while driving drunk (vehicular homicide). He's not in jail for the rest of his life, forced to dwell every day on the person or persons he injured or killed.

There is a really important point here, because even with all of the DUI penalties and improved enforcement, **one-third of fatalities in the US still involve alcohol.** Either stay home; take a cab, Uber, or Lyft; or get someone sober to drive you home.

An interesting aside to this conversation is a recent event that happened to me. While listening to a band where my daughter works (the Georgia Theatre in Athens, Georgia; you should go!), I called for an Uber to give me a ride home. However, that Uber was erroneously taken by a really drunk dude with apparently the same first name as mine. No harm, no foul. My wife called for another Uber on her phone, and we got home okay with the intention of straightening it out with Uber the next morning. In the meantime, I received an email with a hefty clean-up fee *because the guy hurled in the Uber driver's car.* Because of the nature of my alleged behavior, waiting until the next day didn't help my case, but Uber and I eventually worked it out. The (admittedly non-safety-related) moral to the story is to get such events straightened out immediately by calling the driver.

Just Because You Can Doesn't Mean You Should: Part 1

This first installment of "Just Because You Can" is aimed at those who choose to drive after drinking alcohol, even though they may be within the legal BAC limit. As a rule of thumb, **the odds of a fatal crash nearly double (odds = 2.0) with every BAC increase of 0.02 percent.**

For most of us, a 0.02 percent BAC is one drink. With two drinks, the odds double again. Those odds are still higher for young drivers. Driving at half of the legal limit (BAC = 0.04 percent) puts you at *four times the risk* (odds = 4.0) compared to driving sober. These are really high odds. That's why some countries, like Germany, have set their legal BAC limit at 0.05 percent for adults. So again, get the most sober person to drive home or take a cab, Uber, or Lyft.

To give you a better sense of the crash risk for differing BAC levels, our friends at NHTSA published an excellent study that includes this table:

BrAC Relative Risk Unadjusted and Adjusted for Age and Gender

BrAC	Unadjusted Risk	Adjusted Risk (Age and Gender)
0.00	1.00	1.00
0.01	0.51	0.54
0.02	0.82	0.85
0.03	1.17	1.20
0.04	1.57	1.60
0.05	2.05	2.07
0.06	2.61	2.61
0.07	3.25	3.22
0.08	3.98	3.93
0.09	4.83	4.73
0.10	5.79	5.64
0.11	6.88	6.67
0.12	8.11	7.82
0.13	9.51	9.11
0.14	11.07	10.56
0.15	12.82	12.18
0.16	14.78	13.97
0.17	16.97	15.96
0.18	19.40	18.17
0.19	22.09	20.60
0.20+	25.08	23.29
Note: (Relative to BrAC = .00)		

A few words of explanation are in order. First, this table considers a sample for all police-reported crashes, *not just fatal crashes*. This is important because the numbers in the chart differ than the ones listed previously. This is because the crashes included are different; it may also be because the data are relatively recent.

Second, you'll notice that in cases in which the level of alcohol is low (say, one drink or less), the odds appear to be less than 1.0. Why do you think that

is? Well, it certainly appears that drivers are *adapting* to the low alcohol levels, probably because they know they have had a drink and are thus driving a little more conservatively. Good for them! However, the risk starts climbing at a BAC of 0.03 percent, with risk increasing significantly beginning around a BAC of 0.04 percent. Again, depending on your weight and gender, that is just a drink or two over the course of an hour.

I'm realistic, though. There's a good chance most of you will forget these increased odds after a night out with friends or when you feel like you don't have any other choice but to drive. But never, never, never drive while over the legal alcohol limit. And if you are going to drive after a glass or two of wine, make a conscious effort to *adapt*. This means driving at a slower speed, paying closer attention, leaving long headways, and avoiding areas with pedestrians. In other words, do everything you can to minimize your risk.

Sometimes You Should Stay Home and Eat Your Cheese Puffs

When I was in college in the 1970s, my roommate, Rick, and I used to smoke weed and eat an entire Pepperidge Farm coconut cake. We would walk to the grocery store, pick one up, and eat it on the way back. It was frozen and meant to be thawed, but it never got to the point where it thawed. I wonder why ...

The moral to the story? When you get to the point where you want to eat half of a frozen cake before it thaws, you might be impaired enough that you don't need to drive. Fortunately, Rick and I were not motivated to drive during these outings, and we could walk. I am guessing that if we were not close enough to walk, we would have just stayed home and eaten brown sugar out of the bag.

Despite the fact that marijuana has been around for a long time, we don't know a whole lot about how it affects driving. We know that at *some* level there is *significant* impairment, but there hasn't been a lot of research into marijuana and driving primarily because it has been illegal, which makes the research hard to perform. Of course, that's all changing with the legalization of medicinal and recreational marijuana in several states and our nation's capital, with more states certainly to follow.

So, here we are: We don't know what the legal marijuana limit should be. Even if we did know, we don't have an effective roadside test to measure it yet, and we don't really know how it interacts with fatigue and other drugs such as alcohol. For example, let's say you consumed alcohol but are below the legal BAC limit—maybe 0.05 percent, or two to three beers, depending on your weight. If you were also smoking pot, we don't know if you are in worse shape at that point as a driver compared to consuming a fourth beer that would have put you over the legal BAC limit.

I've heard talking heads claim that we're already seeing an increase in crashes due to the legalization of marijuana in some states, and a relatively quick internet search for "increased crashes marijuana" will bring up several reports that seem to verify this claim. However, I have also seen reports that find the injury/crash rate has *not* changed since the legalization of marijuana. A few examples of these varied reports can be found in the References section at the end of this book. What is becoming increasingly obvious is that advocates on both sides of the issue can find numbers to support their individual stances.

In February 2015 NHTSA released results from a study that sought to determine the crash risk of drug- and alcohol-impaired driving compared to a control group of drivers. This study put the odds of a crash risk while under the influence of marijuana between 1.00 and 1.05. Drivers who tested positive for any legal or illegal drugs, but no alcohol, saw odds of 1.02. It should be noted that all of these studies tested the bloodstream for the active ingredient in marijuana, THC. I need to make two points regarding testing for THC:

1. The THC level doesn't necessarily correlate with how impaired your driving is.
2. Unlike alcohol, THC remains in your bloodstream for a very long time, even days or weeks. (This, of course, is why football players and others take "wizzinators" to pass drug tests for marijuana.)

The upshot is that some drivers tested in the NHTSA study could have been stoned *three days prior* and still tested positive for THC. Obviously, the driver is not still impaired at this point, yet he or she is classified as "drug positive" in the results. This is undoubtedly why the odds are closer than one might expect to a risk of 1.0. In fact, they could be much higher, but my point is that we won't know this for sure until we have a much better understanding of the risks of marijuana and driving. Our friends at the Insurance Institute for Highway Safety (IIHS) recently found that crash rates increased an average of about 6 percent following the legalization of marijuana in certain states. However, these findings are only preliminary because drugs like marijuana, unlike alcohol, are not tested for post-crash. The increase could be (and probably is) due in part to factors that go beyond the change in the law.

At VTTI we are trying to help fill this gap in knowledge by conducting naturalistic driving studies specifically focused on the effects of marijuana use as it relates to driver risk. We recently wrapped up the first such study of its kind, which involved about 30 drivers in Colorado. While this is a small-scale study, it's an important step forward in determining the effects of marijuana on drivers in the real world. Our researchers found that, even though drivers experienced a delayed reaction time, the effect was minor. Overall, the effects on drivers who used marijuana were minimal. While the study did not consider the effects of alcohol mixed with marijuana, our findings suggest that THC use in general is certainly not going to create bumper cars out there.

Many questions about marijuana use will take a long time to answer. If you are a policymaker, please fund our marijuana and driving research (just kidding ... sort of). And yes, we need simulator and survey studies to complement such research. Some of the following research questions need to be answered: What happens when alcohol use is the primary impairment versus when marijuana use is the primary impairment? Does marijuana lead to other risks, such as increased distraction or fatigue? It may sound funny, but overadaptation and driving too slowly are possibilities with respect to marijuana.

Until we have more research conducted in the context of actual driving, we simply won't be able to make definitive statements about the impact of marijuana use on driving. Based on my own (unscientific) observations, however, I tend to believe that drivers can adapt better to their driving state under the influence of marijuana than tequila! I say this because I just don't see many crashes occurring at more than 100 mph with marijuana-impaired drivers as opposed to alcohol-impaired drivers. Marijuana-impaired drivers don't seem to drive aggressively in general. There is an old joke: Did you hear about the two stoners in a bar who bumped into each other and got into a fight? Of course not, they were too busy apologizing!

Unfortunately, all of this means that I am not in a position at this time to estimate your risk of crashing when driving under the influence of marijuana. This will no doubt change in the next few years, so stay tuned. In the meantime, I will give you a few words of advice about how to approach the use of marijuana with respect to driving:

1. **Treat marijuana like alcohol.** As our friends at NHTSA say, "If you feel different, you drive different." Stay home; take a cab, Uber, or Lyft; or get someone sober to drive.
2. **Marijuana today is a stronger drug than it used to be, so don't underestimate it!** It takes very little time or energy to get really stoned. Just a couple of puffs or vapes can really get you there. There are also many edible choices that can have both strong and long-lasting effects, even longer than alcohol. Plan accordingly if you take a trip to the Green Planet in Denver or the Bulldog in Amsterdam.

6. Be Attentive and Alert

I was once in Key West watching the street performers down by the water-front. I remember one performer commenting on the risky nature of his job as he was standing on top of an aluminum pole (not attached to anything) while juggling five flaming batons. He said he didn't want to die while per-forming. Rather, he said he wanted to die as his grandfather did—"peacefully, in his sleep ... not like his passengers." The "joke" was that the performer's grandfather fell asleep at the wheel.

It will come as no surprise to you that driving while drowsy leads to impair-ment and crashes. For many years, however, the problem was mostly associ-ated with long-haul truckers, with fatigue being a key ingredient in about 20 percent of truck crashes. Among light vehicles, crashes due to drowsy dri-ving were initially thought to be in the range of 4 to 8 percent. Today, though, we have a growing body of naturalistic and crash data showing fatigue to be an all-vehicle problem, including cars, small trucks, and buses/motor coaches. Specifically, **fatal crashes involve drowsiness about 15 to 20 per-cent of the time.**

The data also show that drowsiness is not limited to the wee hours of the morning, although that is certainly a peak time. Light-vehicle drivers suffer drowsiness symptoms during long morning commutes and in the early after-noon as well. Short-haul truck drivers (think beer or potato chip trucks) tend to be fatigued the most on Mondays, after experiencing some sleep loss over the weekend.

For long-haul trucks, the same trends hold true. Drowsiness can occur dur-ing all times of the day, with several peak times. VTTI researchers performed a study in the late 1990s that examined drowsiness in single and team long-haul drivers. The results showed that **at pretty much any time of the day or night, about 4 percent of truck drivers are falling asleep at the wheel.** We're talking head-bobbing, eye-rubbing, truck-weaving types of falling asleep. That sounds like a pretty small percentage until you begin to count the num-ber of trucks you encounter on your next family vacation. The interstate nearest my house, I-81, has periods during which traffic is more than 50 per-cent trucks. It is common for me to encounter more than 100 trucks during a four-hour drive to Washington, DC. On average, such a trip puts me in close proximity every hour to a 40-ton vehicle where the driver is falling asleep at the wheel! It's a scary thought but is one more reason to **stay away from trucks**. As I've said elsewhere in this book, if you are going to pass a truck, risk a small ticket and pass it briskly.

Regardless of the vehicle you drive, **your crash risk increases at least 2 times with any level of drowsiness (odds = 2.0) and between 4 to 40 times (odds = 4.0–40.0) when you drive at a "moderately" drowsy level or higher, depending on how tired you are**. A moderate level of drowsiness is when you are beginning to struggle to stay awake and find yourself yawning, rubbing your face, and moving around in the seat more than normal. Another important symptom of drowsiness is what we call slow eyelid closures. Unlike a quick blink, a slow closure is like it sounds: the eyelid droops slowly over the eye and then is opened. If you experience slow eyelid closures and perhaps head nods, it's past time to find a safe place to pull over and rest. After all, it's hard to drive with your eyes closed.

My colleague Justin Owens, who works in the VTTI Center for Vulnerable Road User Safety, recently led a study using our largest naturalistic driving database (3,500 drivers) to determine the presence of drowsy driving. The results showed that in nearly 10 percent of crash cases, drowsy driving was a factor, with driver risk **increasing up to 3.8 times (odds = 3.8)** due to drowsy driving.

For my master's thesis, I studied the causes of drowsiness while driving. With the help of my adviser, Walt Wierwille, and lab mate Lenora Hardee, we set out to see if we could develop algorithms that detected when a driver first became drowsy and to warn that driver via a chime and "telltale" icon on the dash that it was time to take a break. The study found that the pattern of sleep onset came in bouts of drowsiness lasting a few minutes followed by a period during which the drivers were able to wake themselves up for a little while. Even though our drivers were sleep deprived, the first bout of drowsiness did not occur for about 15 or 20 minutes. With each successive bout of drowsiness, the amount of recovery time declined and the time between bouts became shorter. These symptoms characterize what we call *sleep inertia*. Simply stated, a body needs sleep. While you can delay the onset of drowsiness for a little while—with coffee, energy drinks, conversation, music, or cold air—the urge and need for sleep will eventually over-whelm those small arousing influences.

What do you do when you feel yourself becoming drowsy while on the road? Frankly, you really don't have many options, and all of them require you to do one thing first—pull off the road immediately! What you do next depends in part on whether you are alone or with other people. If you are alone, your best, and often only, bet is to take a nap. If you are not alone, you can turn the driving over to another person in the car. *However*, this only works if you have someone else with you who is (a) licensed to drive, (b) more alert than you, and (c) willing to take the wheel. If any one of these three things is not the case, then do yourself a favor and take a nap.

My good friends Bob and Rick once traveled cross-country to Boston. Because Bob had just been at a party, Rick took the wheel first when they began driving at midnight, leaving Bob to sleep in the back. As Bob recalled, dawn was just breaking when he was roused from his slumber by the sound of the car hitting gravel and Rick muttering that he couldn't stay awake anymore. Rick pulled over to let Bob take the wheel. Bob said he was fine, although he was clearly still in the process of waking up. Rick climbed into the back of the car, and off they went. About 15 minutes later, Bob was enjoy-ing the nice, warm sun on the car ... a little too much. As Bob said, it was like the scene in *National Lampoon's Vacation* when the Griswolds were all asleep in the Truckster, including Clark, the driver.

Bob quickly woke up when he mowed into a small pole. He yanked the wheel and jammed on the brakes, sending the car into a 360-degree spin. Rick was snapped out of his dreams by the sound of the squealing tires and sat up just in time to catch the flash of an abutment passing by. They managed to come to a halt pointing in the right direction, so Bob dropped the car into first gear and started driving again. Apparently, Rick didn't agree that Bob was fit to continue driving, so they changed shifts again. They both made it to their destination, wide awake and ready for action. The point here is that the nap you take must overcome the sleep inertia, meaning you need to allot time for both the nap and to wake up!

Anyone is susceptible to sleep inertia while driving, but some people are more susceptible than others. According to the Centers for Disease Control and Prevention (CDC), more than 70 million folks in the US suffer from some type of sleep disorder, such as sleep apnea. You may have sleep apnea and not be aware of it. If you are a male, one quick way to tell if you may be at risk of sleep apnea is to measure your neck size. If it's 17 inches or more, there's a good chance you have sleep apnea. If you snore a lot or people tell you it sounds like you stopped breathing when you snore, you may have sleep apnea. If any of this sounds familiar, consider consulting your doctor to find appropriate treatments. There are also the garden-variety insomniacs, like me, who spend hours awake in the middle of the night thinking about how to write a book ...

The important point here is that, for some, sleep inertia can come on quick and hard. You need to pay attention to your alertness level, take a nap when you need it, and get to your destination in one piece with no scratches on your car (or worse!).

Distracted Driving Versus Engaged Driving (or Pay Attention!)

We now know more about driver behavior than ever before. Much of this is due to the advent of naturalistic driving studies. You'll remember that naturalistic driving studies enable researchers to observe volunteer drivers while in the act of driving. What makes this observation possible is a suite of inconspicuously placed cameras, sensors, and radar. Thanks to these studies, researchers can finally see what drivers are doing during the seconds leading up to a crash or near crash. This information allows us to estimate the risk involved in engaging in secondary tasks, such as eating a burger, dialing a phone, reading the newspaper, or applying makeup, while driving. Out of this research comes the notion of "engaged driving."

What is engaged driving? In essence, it means staying focused on driving and avoiding distraction. Our friends at State Farm convened a panel of experts to write a series of papers on engaged driving back in 2014. I participated in the panel, along with my friend, former student, and colleague Charlie Klauer, who heads our VTTI teen-driving research. I wrote one of the papers based on data gathered from four of our naturalistic driving studies. These studies focused specifically on adults, teens, trucks, and cell phone use. Some odds from this paper are included in the next section of this chapter.

One major finding of these studies was that distraction is a key ingredient in all types of crashes. While this might not sound like news, the fact is that distraction as a cause of crashes has been underestimated for many years, similar to the way drowsiness was (and still is) underestimated among car drivers. Naturalistic driving studies show that, more than 50 percent of the time, drivers are doing something else while driving. The primary reason that previous studies underestimated distraction is that it's nearly impossible to accurately determine the presence of distraction based on police crash investigations. After a crash, drivers can be dead, injured, or dazed, may not remember what happened, or may be lying about what actually happened. What percentage of drivers who are involved in a crash while using their phones will admit doing so to an investigating officer? I would guess that it's in the ballpark of 50 percent.

Eyes Forward, Hands on the Wheel

All of the VTTI naturalistic studies, as well as similar studies conducted elsewhere, show a recurring theme. The greatest distraction-related crash risks occur when the driver's eyes look away from the road ahead, for whatever reason, in conjunction with an unexpected event happening simultaneously. In other words, a crash is imminent if both these key ingredients are present to make our figurative cake. If I could give you one piece of general advice about driving safety, it would be to **keep your eyes on the road!**

Visual distraction is nothing new. For many years, the classic example was manually tuning a radio. Most of us with a good bit of mileage probably know someone who had a crash or near crash while tuning a radio, inserting a CD, or plugging in/changing the music on an iPod. I know a few.

One peculiar example of a crash caused by visual distraction involved my good friend Bob, who was traveling on an unfamiliar road at night in his VW Beetle. While looking down to find a good radio station, Bob missed a sharp turn. His car launched onto a large shrub, with all four wheels off of the ground. If that wasn't bad enough, when Bob landed on the shrub, the muffler of his car got knocked off and his hand knocked the blaring aftermarket radio out of the dash and into the trunk (the engine was in back). The radio wasn't wired through the ignition and the car was high enough off the ground that Bob, unfortunately, couldn't get into the trunk to turn down the radio. His blaring radio made it difficult to go unnoticed, even in a very rural location. Eventually, Bob was able to turn off the radio and get a ride home, only to have a visit from the local sheriff the next morning.

Visual distraction has become an even greater concern now that we have wireless devices like smartphones to draw our attention away from driving. The fact that smartphones are even called phones anymore is really a misnomer; you can do so many very distracting things with them outside of just making a call.

One of the best ways to stay focused on the road is to mind your inner clock. More specifically, you need to develop an alarm in your head that goes off any time you look away from the road for more than two seconds. If you are able to do this consistently, **you will *halve* your crash risk. Put another way, you double your risk of crashing when you look away from the road for more than two seconds.**

Our friends at NHTSA and the Auto Alliance both agree with this two-second rule. The graph below from a VTTI study illustrates the point, with the x-axis indicating seconds and the y-axis indicating your odds of crashing.

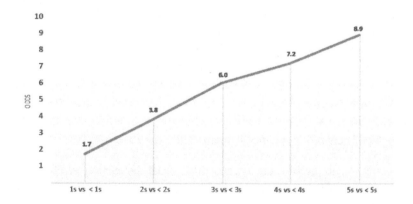

The level of risk if you take your eyes off the forward roadway longer than two seconds.

Here's a tip to practice while you are driving: when you choose to do something outside of the main driving task, count "thousand one, thousand two" and see if your eyes are back on the road. Do the same when you are riding with others, especially younger drivers, and provide them with this sage advice. Even though your advanced knowledge of driving safety may seem unappreciated at the time, those you tell will at least think about this two-second rule and may even begin to do it. You also need to avoid looking away from the road more than a few times while performing a nondriving task. This is another dimension to the "eyes-off-the-road" rule that you need to think about. Pay attention to the number of times you look away from the road, even when you are looking away for short periods of time.

Even with short glances away from the road, your awareness of your surroundings decreases. The probability of a crash occurring due to an unexpected event increases with each glance away from the road. The work conducted at VTTI continuously proves the point that **taking your eyes off the road for more than six seconds, even in multiple short glances, begins to significantly increase your crash risk.**

If you follow the two-second rule advice, this means taking three glances away from the forward roadway. I would say this is the *maximum* amount of time you should take your eyes away from the road, but such time also greatly depends on where you are driving. If you're on a rural interstate in Kansas on a sunny, dry day with no other traffic around, you are probably okay taking a few short glances that total 10 or 12 seconds. If you are on the Washington, DC, beltway in heavy traffic during a torrential rainstorm, just wait until you are stopped or are safely at home before you perform any secondary task that takes your eyes off the road *at all*. (Remember: *adapt!*)

With all of this information in mind, the following numbers provide some "best-guess" crash risk estimates for common secondary (that is, distracting) tasks performed while driving. The data are based on the State Farm paper I mentioned above. While these numbers may change as we get more data, I doubt they will change much, and I don't expect the factors shown as being the most or least risky will change at all.

Best-guess odds of crashing while "doing other stuff" at the same time

	Adult	Distracted Teen vs. Attentive Teen	Distracted Teen vs. Attentive Adult
Cell texting	5.0	6.0	10.0
Cell dialing	5.0	5.0	6.0
Cell reaching	4.0	6.0	8.0
Cell browsing	3.5	4.5	5.5
Cell talking	1.5	2.0	2.5
Talking on handheld	2.2	N/A	N/A
Talking on hands-free	1.0 (maybe less!)	1.0+	1.0+
Vehicle (radio, A/C, etc.)	1.5	2.5	3.0
Reading (paper map, other)	10.0	8.0	12.0
Applying makeup	2.0	4.0	6.0
Eating	1.5	3.0	4.0
Drinking (nonalcohol)	1.3	2.5	3.0
Actively talking to passenger	1.2	2.0	2.5
Looking at outside object, person, etc.	5.0	8.0	12.0
Dispatching device (commercial drivers only)	10.0	N/A	N/A

Several points are worth making here:

1. **You can't drive safely if you aren't looking at the road.** Visual tasks that may also require a manual component, or what we call visual/manual secondary tasks, have the highest crash risk. This includes dialing, texting, reaching for a phone or any other object, or reading.

2. **Talking on a cell phone can be a distracting secondary task, depending on your use of a handheld or hands-free phone.** As you probably noted in the chart above, there is a difference in risk between talking on a *handheld* phone and talking on a (well-designed) *hands-free* phone, with the latter actually showing a protective effect (that is, an odds of less than

1.0), at least relative to adult drivers. This probably has to do with the act of holding the phone, which of course is absent when talking on a hands-free phone. The act of holding the phone means drivers only have one hand on the wheel, making maneuvers more difficult. Holding the phone to one's ears also decreases one's searching and scanning abilities.

3. **Teens are susceptible to more types of distractions than adults.** Eating, drinking, interacting with passengers, and using the A/C or radio appear to be somewhat higher-risk scenarios for teens when compared to adults. This suggests the driving task itself requires more attention from teens because they are new at it. Consequently, teens are more likely than adults to get sucked into the secondary tasks and forget about the primary task–*driving!* The very fact that teens start out with a crash rate three times higher than adults further highlights how risky secondary tasks are for teens.

4. **The distraction effect is not nearly as large for any of the drivers for tasks that require very few glances away from the road.** Which brings us to our next topic ...

What About My Talking Car and My Talking Phone?

Drivers can now perform numerous tasks hands-free via Bluetooth or other built-in systems. The most popular task is probably navigation, but you can also manipulate the temperature, radio, messaging, etc., of the vehicle via voice-only interactions. However, it's essential that any hands-free system you use is *well-designed.* A critical component of a well-designed hands-free system is that it uses voice instead of a visual display to communicate information back to you. Again, looking at the road is critical. Anything you can do to keep your eyes on the road while driving will reduce your crash risk.

Plenty of studies show no benefit to using a poorly designed hands-free operation when compared to performing the same task manually and visually. One such study conducted by VTTI in the late 1990s by Andy Gellatly, a former student, supported this conclusion. The study was designed to assess an earlier version of voice dialing. The system was inaccurate to the point where the driver had to look at the dashboard after voicing every number to see if the system had entered the number correctly. If the number was wrong, the driver had to manually correct it. The study also found that the faulty voice command system actually created *more* risk than manual dialing because it took the driver's eyes off the road more than manual dialing!

Wait, Where Am I?

Distraction isn't always visual. Your mind can easily wander and get lost in thought. All of this falls under the umbrella of what we call *cognitive distraction*. Generally speaking, cognitive distraction does not place visual/manual demands on the driver. A driver may have his or her eyes on the forward roadway but may be *thinking* about (not actively *doing*) something else. The concept probably isn't new to you; many of us spend a lot of time in a car, and driving is often mundane, so we do many things to keep our minds occupied. We make phone calls; truckers use CB radios; we listen to audiobooks, music, news, conversations, and podcasts. In fact, **more than 50 percent of the time, drivers are doing something in addition to driving. The percentage increases to 70 percent just prior to crashes.**

At VTTI we analyze a lot of video of people crashing in real-world settings. Thanks to our naturalistic driving studies, we have captured more than 2,000 crashes using multicamera systems that typically involve four to five cameras. In these videos, rarely do we see a case during which someone is looking directly at something and runs into it. (Although, on occasion, we do see someone miss a traffic signal or stop sign.) By contrast, we see hundreds of cases involving drivers engaged in visual/manual distractions who take their eyes off the road and then subsequently crash. This indicates that, relatively speaking, cognitive distraction is less risky than visual/manual distraction.

How "less risky" is cognitive distraction? At VTTI we have worked on several studies trying to answer this very question. In one study we tried to determine how prevalent cognitive distraction was among drivers. To do this, we focused on secondary tasks that can be considered mainly cognitive in nature: talking or singing alone or with a passenger, talking or listening on a handheld cell phone, talking or listening on a hands-free cell phone, and dialing hands-free using voice-activated software. We found that drivers were engaged in such cognitive secondary tasks about 20 percent of the time while driving. However, we also found that engaging in such tasks did not generally increase crash risk compared to everyday driving (although the risk went up slightly when only compared to alert, attentive, and sober drivers, but it's important to keep in mind that crash risk will typically always be higher when comparing to this group because they represent the "best of the best" cases—what we call model driving—on the road).

In another VTTI study, we attempted to understand the degree to which "cognitive disengagement" leads to crashes. Cognitive disengagement includes cases in which the driver may be "zoned out" and not thinking about driving at all. During this study, we assessed three types of cognitive disengagement: (1) purely cognitive distraction, where the driver was performing a cognitive secondary task and did not look away from the road; (2) mind wandering, where the driver was just thinking about something else; and (3) a small amount of fatigue called microsleep. We analyzed only the cases where no other figurative cake ingredient was present—like texting or looking away from the road longer than two seconds—but the driver's reaction to the crash showed signs that he or she was not cognitively engaged with the driving task, such as a slow brake reaction time.

What did we find here? Well, we determined that less than 1 percent of crashes examined had mind wandering or microsleep as a main ingredient in the crash; about 1.5 percent of crashes had purely cognitive distraction as a main ingredient. That's not to say cognitive distraction was altogether absent in crashes; rather, cognitive distraction was not found to be a primary factor in the crash. More often than not, for all the thousands of crashes we have seen, the crash was primarily due to the driver looking away from the forward road because he or she was visually or manually distracted by something else or because the driver was nodding off at the wheel.

Obviously, anything that presents some kind of risk to the driver is a safety issue. However, relative to visual/manual distraction or fatigue, cognitive distraction does not appear to present that much of a risk.

Along these lines, you may hear that talking on any kind of cell phone is considered a form of cognitive distraction because your eyes are on the road compared to when you are, say, texting. You may hear that performing such a task is significantly risky to you as a driver. However, there are a few bits of information to keep in mind here. **If you are an adult driver, the risk of crashing while talking on a handheld cell phone is about 1.5 (odds = 1.5). For novice drivers, the risk increases to about 2.5 (odds = 2.5). If you are texting**

on a phone while driving, your crash risk increases between 4.0 and 23.0 times (odds = 4.0–23.0), depending on vehicle type and driver.

Yes, a handheld cell phone conversation does increase your crash risk. However, if you're wondering to yourself, "Wait, these are *handheld* phone conversations; isn't the *handheld* part a manual task in some sense?" I would reply, "Hold on a minute ..."

An interesting study performed by our friends at the IIHS used the VTTI 100-Car Naturalistic Driving Study data to determine that engaging in cell phone conversations while driving does not significantly increase crash risk. The IIHS made this statement because drivers typically cognitively disengage from driving simply by doing *something*, even if they aren't involved in a cell phone conversation. It has become popular to debate the risk of a cell conversation while driving as a main type of cognitive distraction. There are advocates you may hear in the news who will say that it's incredibly risky. They will argue that a cell phone conversation can be more "emotional" or that the driver is compelled to keep the phone conversation going even when driving demands 100 percent attention because the other person is not in the driving "context" and to interrupt the conversation seems "rude" to the driver. I would counter by saying that lumping all types of cell phone conversation into one general statement—that talking on a cell phone is dangerous to you as a driver—is misleading.

For example, the VTTI cognitive studies found that talking or listening on a *hands-free* cell phone did *not* increase driver risk. In fact, we found *zero crashes* in the largest naturalistic driving study ever conducted (3,500 drivers for up to two years) associated with having a hands-free phone conversation. Now, what about having a conversation on a *handheld* phone? That is where we see increased risk—presumably because the very act of talking on a handheld phone requires holding the phone, thereby leaving the driver with one hand on the wheel and decreased ability to visually scan his or her driving environment.

The great state of Georgia (which is suddenly a bastion of driving safety; congratulations to all of you, including your lawmakers) recently passed a hands-free law, meaning that it's illegal to talk, browse, or text on any handheld device while driving. We have been advocating for such laws for almost 20 years! Thus far, the initial crash stats coming out of Georgia back up our assertions. In 2018 the Georgia State Patrol reported that traffic crashes declined following implementation of the hands-free law—crashes were down nearly 9 percent in August 2018 compared to August 2017. Overall, the state reported a decline in crash fatalities by 11 percent year-to-date, the largest decrease in a decade.

The last time I was in Georgia visiting my daughter, Emily, I was surprised to see that she would not let herself pick up a phone while driving, for any reason, due to the hands-free law. I was even more surprised when several of her friends, both male and female, followed suit. That's a small sample for sure; however, given that they are all in the 23–25 age range, it's certainly a good sign!

If you see advocacy groups post or talk about how much riskier cognitive distraction is compared to visual/manual distraction, please keep this chapter in mind. There's no question that the number 1 problem in transportation safety is drivers taking their **eyes off the forward road**. However, cognitive distraction is still something to which we should pay attention (pun intended). With this in mind, I advise the following to keep you safe and to minimize your risk of experiencing cognitive distraction: as a driver, stick to your primary task. One trap that many drivers fall into, particularly novice or young drivers, is forgetting which of the two (or three, or four) things they are doing is most important. For example, a cell phone conversation should always be the *secondary* task when you are driving. Talking should only be engaged in while driving under ideal conditions, when traffic is light and when weather conditions permit. If such driving conditions change—or if you feel yourself getting sucked into the conversation emotionally (remember, driving while visibly emotional can also increase your crash risk)—interrupt the conversation and tell mom, dad, or junior that you'll call back later. Other examples of tasks that are always secondary in nature while driving are listening to music and eating in the car. If situations in the driving environment become bad or difficult, turn off the stereo, put down the cheese fries, and adapt to survive.

Navigating Is a Necessary Part of the Driving Task

At this point, you may be asking yourself, What's wrong with this guy? I have this TV in the dash of my new Tesla with a map on it, and he's not even talking about how distracting it is! To which I say, yes, but have you considered that navigating to a destination is (presumably) not a secondary task because you need to know how to get there so you can, in fact, get there? When it comes to navigating, there is significant risk in the form of more road time (exposure), missed turns, or searching for signs when you are lost. Navigating is a necessary part of the driving task.

For my PhD dissertation in 1985 I conducted the first on-road investigation of the safety associated with the use of an in-car navigation system. With the help of my adviser and lab mates, we designed an early prototype of an instrumented vehicle with cameras and other sensors that measured real-world driving performance. A photo is shown here of that first instrumentation, which became the basis for the VTTI naturalistic driving study research method.

Early transportation research instrumentation, which became the basis for the VTTI naturalistic driving study research method (left). Newer instrumentation that captures a view of the driver's face, which can tell us a lot about driver behavior in the real world (right).

This setup doesn't look all that sophisticated today, but in 1985 it was beyond state of the art. In fact, the systems we build now are slightly larger than a box of playing cards and much more capable than my 1985 version. At the time the concept of an in-car navigation system was quite new, which meant that we had no way of knowing what the safety implications were. Given that navigation was an essential part of the driving task, the question for this study then became, What is the best way to navigate safely while driving?

After performing the main study described above and several others, including a study in the mid-1990s I conducted with my friend and former student Dan McGehee, using 100 vehicles in Orlando, we found the following:

1. Moving maps that are *well-designed* are less visually demanding than paper maps or direction lists.
2. Turn-by-turn screens are less visually demanding than moving maps.
3. Adding *well-designed* voice commands to either moving maps or turn-by-turn screens reduce the visual demand placed on the driver.
4. If they work well, voice commands alone are the least visually demanding option.

Notice in the last result that I said voice commands alone are the least visually demanding, not the least distracting. This is because, again, navigation is part of the driving task. Essentially, if you have a *well-designed* voice navigation system, your risk is reduced compared to any other navigation option available.

Speaking of Attentive and Alert ... A Few Tips for Commercial Drivers

Long-haul trucks constitute only about 10 percent of trucks on the road today. Commercial trucks that make shorter (local/short-haul) deliveries are more common.

As I was writing this book, I struggled at times to decide what to include and not to include. For instance, I wasn't sure what to say about long-haul or line-haul (that is, *big*) trucks. I opted not to include heavy trucks from the trucker's viewpoint, primarily because the subject is so vast that it could turn into its own book. The truth is that truck driving is *very* different from "four-wheel" driving. Truck drivers have special training; special licenses, such as the commercial driver's license; special regulations that include hours of service; differing laws, such as zero tolerance for alcohol; different medical requirements; and a different lifestyle that leads to sleep- and health-related issues, among others. Someday, I may work with my truck and bus colleagues to write a book about heavy trucks, if this book does okay.

Although we all think of the big long-haul semi-tractor trailers when we first think of trucks, they actually constitute only about 10 percent of the trucks on the road today. There are many other commercial trucks that make shorter deliveries. These local or short-haul trucks do not have to adhere to many of the same requirements as interstate trucks. In addition, there are many, many people in the US and around the world whose job it is to drive a vehicle other than a truck for a living. Think of taxis and limousines, to name just two.

If you drive for a living, congratulations! You have one of the most dangerous occupations in the United States! If you are a farmer, rancher, logger, or construction worker and you say, "No way," I have news for you. Many risks occur while you are in, or driving, a vehicle. In some cases, professional drivers rival commercial fishing for the top spot as the most dangerous occupation.

A big reason for your on-the-job risk as a professional driver is your *exposure*. Throughout this book, you have seen the phrases "crash *rate*" or "fatal crash *rate*" numerous times. The rate is typically per mile traveled; even when the rate is low, your risk still increases with every mile you drive. And many of you professional drivers cover a lot of miles. This makes much of the advice in this book even more important for you.

So, here are just a few tips I want to pass along:

1. While many of you get paid by the mile or trip, don't let the money or job pressure make you lose sight of the consequences of your actions while driving. Some of you carry perishable goods that need to be delivered in a shorter timeframe than other types of cargo. Some of you are supposed to make a very large number of sales calls every day, which means you are more or less expected to work while you drive. Some of you have to meet an arbitrary deadline, such as, "Will be delivered in 30 minutes or less, or your pizza is free." Many of you get paid more money

if you can make more trips in the same amount of time. These rules incentivize professional drivers to drive while distracted, drive while drowsy, drive as fast as possible, or drive aggressively. As a professional driver, you must avoid these traps—for your own safety and the safety of others.

2. Even though you have a high level of practice and skill, you still have to look at the road. I have been involved in a number of legal cases and have given congressional testimony about driving distraction. I have heard arguments that commercial drivers are highly skilled and so well trained that they can drive while doing other things like reading, writing, or interacting with dispatching devices. Rich Hanowski and his colleagues in the VTTI Center for Truck and Bus Safety have found that, after cell phone texting, interacting with electronic dispatching devices is the riskiest activity for commercial drivers. **When a commercial driver is using a dispatching device, he or she is at 10 times greater risk (odds = 10.0) than when just driving.** Many of you need to use such devices while driving to get your next load or fare, and I get that. But some of these devices are poorly designed and require you to take your eyes off the road for too long. Focus on finding ways to do what you need to do with as few short glances (remember, less than two seconds) away from the road as possible. If the message on your dispatching device is long or you have to type, it's imperative that you pull over in a safe spot to read or type.

3. No matter how much experience or skill you have, you can't drive safely when you look away from the road frequently or for long periods of time. Take a look at this chapter for more details about what is and isn't okay when it comes to driving distraction; the risks outlined there apply to professional drivers too.

4. Fatigue is a serious issue for many professional drivers. Most of you aren't regulated for hours of service, and many of you work long shifts. This puts you at greater risk for drowsiness than private vehicle drivers. Remember, if you are tired enough to experience slow eyelid closures or head bobbing, you just have to take a break and, preferably, a nap.

7. Aggressive Driving 101

Be Kind and Caring

It's not just you on the road. It's you plus over 220 million other licensed drivers in the US alone (not to mention unlicensed drivers), as well as bicyclists, pedestrians, wildlife, and more. In this chapter, I will offer some informed advice on how to drive more peacefully and safely while you are sharing the road with others.

Make Love, Not War

Aggressive driving has become a serious issue in the United States—so much so that NHTSA has funded studies devoted specifically to finding ways to curb it. (See the reference list at the end of the book.) According to NHTSA, aggressive driving is "The operation of a motor vehicle in a manner that endangers or is likely to endanger persons or property." We have all seen examples of aggressive driving on the road. Think of the times you've been on the interstate and marveled at drivers tailgating at 70 mph or weaving in and out of traffic with very close spacing. Most of these offenders are men, and most of them are younger men, which supports my point about testosterone in chapter 5.

Our friends at the AAA Foundation for Traffic Safety estimate that **more than half of all fatal crashes involve at least one aggressive driver.** Of those fatal crashes, about two-thirds involve excessive speeding. In short, a lot of people are killed on the road because others are in too much of a hurry to operate a vehicle safely within traffic and road conditions.

Thanks to a late 1990s study at the University of Michigan by my colleagues Bob Ervin and Paul Fancher, I came to understand this kind of behavior better. The subject of their study was adaptive cruise control. Adaptive cruise control allows you to set your following *distance*, as opposed to regular cruise control, which lets you only set your following *speed*. Adaptive cruise control uses radar to set your headway to the vehicle in front, keeping you at a constant distance from the car ahead. Once you have clear space in front of you, the vehicle returns to the set speed, just like cruise control. Using the data generated from this radar, Bob and Paul found that drivers usually fall into one of two groups: "hunters" and "gliders." Hunters are always pushing the limit, trying to find a faster way to get to where they're going. Gliders are generally happy to go with the flow of traffic. I must confess that I am a hunter, but I wish I were a glider because, frankly, the gliders I know usually get to their destination nearly as fast as I do but with much less stress. Of course, being a hunter does not necessarily make you a bad driver. The problem comes when a hunter is overly aggressive, because overly aggressive drivers put themselves—and others—in danger.

An example of an aggressive driver is a male (again, aggressive drivers are typically male) traveling on a congested four-lane highway, weaving in and out of traffic at very close spacing to get to wherever he is headed. However, he arrives only a minute or two earlier than he hoped because the traffic volume was such that driving aggressively made little to no difference. Other characteristic signs of an aggressive driver include passing a bicycle at a close distance or passing a car on a two-way road with too short of a sight distance.

Like It or Not, Driving Is a Social Endeavor

Bill Murray summed it up best when he said to his truck-wielding groundhog companion in *Groundhog Day*, "Don't drive angry. Don't drive angry!" And Bill was right. Research performed at VTTI shows that **driving angry or in some other elevated emotional state increases your crash risk by nearly 10 times (odds = 10.0) compared to normal driving.**

There will always be hunters on the road; this is a simple fact of life. However, even hunters can learn when to chill out—when to not become aggressive and put us all in danger. Take me as an example: I may have needed 25 years, but eventually I learned that all of my efforts to get ahead in traffic ultimately didn't speed things up that much. This doesn't mean you shouldn't plan ahead and look for ways to shorten your trip. It really just means you should avoid the temptation to engage in extreme driving behavior.

For those of you who are gliders, there are a few simple things you can do to lessen the dangers associated with aggressive driving.

Bill Murray was right when he told his furry companion in Groundhog Day, "Don't drive angry. Don't drive angry!"

Let's face it, you are sharing the road with hunters, and they care much more than you do about getting to their destinations quickly–so get out of their way. For instance, nothing drives hunters crazier than gliders who stay in the left lane with their cruise control set on 70.001 mph while traffic in the right lane is going 70.000 mph. The left lane used to be, and still is in many countries, the *fast* or *passing* lane. For example, hang out in the left lane in Germany and see what happens. All drivers should move into the left lane to pass briskly (especially around trucks) and then move back into the right lane once they have passed. I need to give a shout-out to my home state of Virginia, as they have recently started putting up variable message signs (the electronic messaging system) that read, "The Left Lane Is for Passing, Not for Cruising." Yay! They display that message because if you're caught lolly-gagging in the left lane in Virginia, you'll be fined $100. I think it should be $10,000, but hey, it's a start for hunters like me.

Another way to help lessen the danger for everyone on the road is to use your turn signal properly. About 10 years ago, VTTI conducted a small survey in the Washington, DC, area. We asked people about their use of turn signals.

What we found was that roughly 57 percent of drivers did not use signals at least part of the time. These drivers gave many reasons for failing to do so, but perhaps my favorite response was "If I signal, other drivers will close the gap I am trying to get into." This is a form of aggressive driving behavior that doesn't help the situation for all drivers on the road. In the long run it's better to be polite. Let others go in front of you; merge out of a closed lane before you get to the end and avoid slowing everyone down. If someone ahead of you uses his or her turn signal, make room for that driver and resist "closing the gap."

If you are often on the receiving end of various pointed gestures from other drivers beyond a hand wave, you should look in the mirror—both the one at home and the rearview mirror in your car. Ultimately, whether you are a hunter or a glider, you may want to think about how much it costs you to exercise a little bit of courtesy on the road. I guarantee it's not much.

My last little piece of socially conscious advice may save you in a more direct way: dim your headlights at night when cars are approaching from the other lane. It seems obvious, but I wish I had a dollar for each time I passed a car or truck with high beams on. If you've put a lift kit on your truck (I am from southwest Virginia, after all), get your headlamps re-aimed.

Vulnerable Road Users

Vulnerable road users is a term used at VTTI and elsewhere to describe those who are essentially unprotected by steel, shatterproof glass, airbags, and crumple zones. Bicyclists and pedestrians are the most vulnerable road users. For obvious reasons, they are more susceptible to injuries and fatalities than those with protection. In recent years, the fatality numbers for vulnerable road users have increased. According to NHTSA, both bicyclist and pedestrian fatalities are on the rise, with the latter seeing a 15 percent jump in just the past decade.

Most pedestrian and bicycle fatality victims are male (70 percent and 88 percent, respectively), and most occur in urban areas (73 percent and 71 percent, respectively). The major risk factors for vulnerable road users are conspicuity (how well the vulnerable road user can be seen) and alcohol. Researchers at VTTI are beginning to focus more on this problem in an effort to assess risky behaviors that pedestrians are performing on their end that may contribute to increased crash risk.

Around 2018 electric scooters, or e-scooters, quickly descended onto the transportation scene as a popular ridesharing option. The concept of scooter-sharing is simple: for next to nothing, you can hop on a scooter you've located via one of several scooter-share programs and zip around a city that allows scooter-sharing. While it's difficult to say exactly how many scooters are out there right now, the most recent data come from Forbes, which estimates 65,000 scooters operating in cities from San Diego to Austin to DC.

The benefits of scooter-sharing programs are real, especially in cities afflicted with traffic congestion. Scooters offer efficient and economical alternatives to get you to your destination (within reason, as city regulations often allow scooter usage within a designated parameter). San Francisco, among other cities, is leveraging the popularity of e-scooters to boost transportation options among low-income populations. These efforts allow scooter-share companies to double their number of scooters on the road *if* they enroll a certain number of individuals on low-income plans.

There are some cons to scooter-sharing, such as scooter riders' potential to become a new type of vulnerable road user. While we don't have good exposure data yet, a UCLA study published in 2019 examined scooter injuries based on patients admitted to two different ERs (Santa Monica and Ronald Reagan UCLA Medical Center) during a one-year span. Of the nearly 250 patients studied, about 230 were scooter riders, with 80 percent of them sustaining injuries from falls, more than 10 percent from striking an object, and nearly 10 percent from being hit by a vehicle or object. Impairment was found to be the cause in about 5 percent of the scooter patient cases. Meanwhile, Atlanta officials have declared a nearly threefold increase in injuries that require medical attention due to scooters. The CDC and others are currently conducting studies to better understand scooter safety risks, which should shed more light on the issue.

Because of the relatively sudden rise of scooter-sharing programs, cities have been scrambling to get coherent policies on the books to address issues such as fixing speed limits, riding on congested downtown sidewalks, and riding while impaired.

The sudden rise of scooter-sharing programs has left many cities scrambling to develop appropriate rules of the road so that scooter users can operate safely alongside other vulnerable and non-vulnerable users.

And then there's the question of helmets. Should cities require them or enforce any existing helmet laws on the books? Though some scooter-sharing programs offer free helmets, most riders do not use them. The UCLA study found that less than 5 percent of the studied scooter riders were wearing a helmet, while the ongoing CDC study has already determined that less than 1 percent of scooter users wear helmets. Still, some cities have actually loosened their helmet laws, with California enacting a law in January 2019 allowing riders 18 and older to go without a helmet.

There's some debate in my business as to the longevity of e-scooters. Are they a fad or are they here to stay? I side with the latter because I believe that e-scooters fill a real need in the world of transportation. They are fast, convenient, and economical. If you've ever ridden one (and didn't get hurt), you probably agree. But frankly, we have to address the safety issues and come to terms with their place in the overall transportation picture. With that in mind, here are a few tips on riding an e-scooter:

1. Always test out the brakes when you first get on.
2. Always make sure both front and rear lights work, even in daylight, to increase conspicuity.
3. Wear a helmet, whether it's your own or one offered by the scooter-sharing program.
4. Ride in bike lanes whenever possible. E-scooters are similar to bikes in

size and speed, and bike lanes offer some level of protection from cars. However, you need to be aware of bikes so you can avoid them and they can avoid you.

5. If no bike lanes or other protected lanes are available, ride on the sidewalk when it is safe to do so. "Safe to do so" means that you can effectively and courteously steer clear of all pedestrians.

6. Ride scooters at generally 10 mph or below. At under 10 mph, most folks can hop off quickly if needed, run along beside the scooter, and then quickly (and safely) come to a stop. At 15 mph ... a face-plant on rough concrete may be in your future.

7. Pay attention to potholes, cracks in sidewalks, small obstacles, and any other possible impediment. Otherwise, that tiny little wheel will flip you off in a heartbeat.

8. Always follow the rules of the road. Just like all travelers, e-scooter riders cannot violate the expectations of other road users or a crash will be inevitable.

One certain way to reduce crashes and fatalities is to separate the vulnerable from the nonvulnerable road users. Sidewalks, bike trails, and bike lanes will always help reduce fatalities. However, if you have to share the road, below are a few tips in doing so safely.

For the Nonvulnerable Users

1. Numerous conflicts and crashes occur because the car driver is treating the vulnerable user like the wrong type of vehicle. Therefore, you need to have a clear mental model of the kind of vulnerable user with whom you are interacting. Here is how I tend to classify vulnerable road users:

    ◦ Bicycle = Runner
    ◦ Electric Bicycle = Bicycle
    ◦ Scooter = Bicycle
    ◦ Motorcycle or Big Scooter = Car

To make a mental model in your head, you should ask yourself a few questions. First, does the vulnerable user have the right to an entire vehicle travel lane, or should he or she be on the shoulder? Second, and just as important, is the vulnerable user actually in a vehicle travel lane or on the shoulder? No matter what, you want to give a wide berth if and when you choose to pass.

2. Be patient; you don't have X-ray vision. When I am talking to bicycle enthusiasts, the complaint I probably hear the most is that drivers tend to pass bicyclists even when there is no way they can see far enough ahead, often cutting too close or cutting off bicyclists.

Share the road with bicyclists—they are among the most vulnerable road users, even on city streets with dedicated bike lanes.

For the Vulnerable Users

1. Obey the rules of the road. Don't violate the expectations of those who could run over you—especially in intersections! Numerous fatalities occur in intersections, so make sure you don't violate signals or run stop signs.

2. Stay focused and always be aware of those around you! Just like everyone else on the road, you need to pay attention to the primary task of biking, walking, or whatever nonvehicular mode of transport you are using.

3. Be conspicuous! Wear reflective or bright-colored clothing. Make sure you have a lot of reflectors on your backpack or bike. Use lights and

flashing lights on your bike, both on the front *and* the back. In general, assume drivers don't see you, because they often don't.

8. Teaching Your Teen to Drive

My friend Doug and I often end up on some kind of adventure with an old car, truck, or trailer (because we are old and pretty cheap). Doug has coined a phrase that we use on such adventures: "We need to avoid our 16-year-old selves." Even at our age, we have a tendency to not do the safe thing: that is, *not* to put a ratchet strap on that mattress in the truck because we are in a hurry; *not* to fix the boat-trailer lights; *not* to worry about the brakes on a trailer carrying a 6,000-pound boat because we can go slow. Okay, it's mostly me who has those tendencies.

The point about avoiding our 16-year-old selves is actually very important. Especially when you consider the risks of 16-year-old drivers, particularly 16-year-old male drivers. They are not adults, and they don't drive like adults. They have not had the life experiences to understand the limitations of being 16 years old, and this puts them at very high risk. Consider the following:

Newly licensed teen drivers are *three times more likely* to get into a fatal crash than their adult counterparts. For the first three months after getting a driver's license, teen drivers are *eight times more likely* to be involved in a crash or a near crash. These are huge, scary, and sad statistics. In fact, teens are more likely to die due to a car crash than they are due to *all* other sources of unintentional injury and disease *combined*. Few teens these days have not been touched by a crash, either directly or indirectly. Most know a friend, acquaintance, or classmate who has been killed in a car wreck. If you are a teen driver, pay attention to this book. If you are a parent or guardian of a teen driver, pay even closer attention, because this is reality. When it comes to driving, your life can completely change—or end—*in one second*.

Over the last decade I have conducted several naturalistic driving studies of newly licensed teens with my colleagues Bruce Simons-Morton, a recent retiree from the National Institutes of Health (NIH), and Charlie Klauer, who oversees our teen research group at VTTI. One of the most important discoveries we made in our studies is that teens are more knowledgeable about driving than we tend to give them credit for. By and large teens know how to handle a vehicle reasonably well, and they know how to drive it safely. The problem is, despite this knowledge, *they often choose not to drive safely*.

This is significant because it sheds light on the age-old debate about teen drivers: Is the problem that they need more or better driver education and training, or is it that they need more or better supervision, age, and maturity? Of course, more or better training will always be helpful, but the reality is that teen drivers are at risk *because they lack maturity and experience*, thus they need more supervision. (Interestingly, a recent article published in *Pediatrics* suggests that states with primary distracted driving laws on the books—that is, police can pull over a driver specifically for violating a distracted driving law, like texting while driving—may be another factor in the safety of teen drivers. In the article, researchers found that **teen driver risk *decreased by one-third* in states with primary distracted driving laws**.)

To illustrate, in one of our studies with Bruce and the NIH, we instrumented the cars of 42 newly licensed teens for 18 months with unobtrusive cameras and sensors. The teens all volunteered for the study. As a result, we were able to gather lots of data from which we drew a number of important conclusions about the behaviors of teen drivers. One part of the study focused on the errors teens make while merging in traffic. We found that, in general, teens make the same number of errors, or fewer, than adults. In other words, teens know and follow the rules—such as using turn signals, matching speed, and checking blind spots—at least as well as adults. Next we measured a number of specific teen driving behaviors, including braking hard, swerving, speeding, and "hitting the gas." At VTTI we call these "risky vehicle-based driving behaviors." The higher the rate of these risky driving behaviors, the higher the likelihood of a crash. As shown in the figure below, teens in this particular study engaged in these behaviors *about four to five times more frequently* than the adults ... except when teens had an adult in the car. With an adult in the car, teens exhibited risky driving behaviors *at about the same rate as the adults.*

The same was true with other types of risky driving behaviors, such as driving while distracted. In other words, teens drove like adults when they were supervised, but they drove like creatures from another planet when adults were not present. This led us to conclude that **most teen drivers know how to drive safely, *but they choose not to.*** (I know I am being repetitive here, but we're big on redundancy in my line of work.)

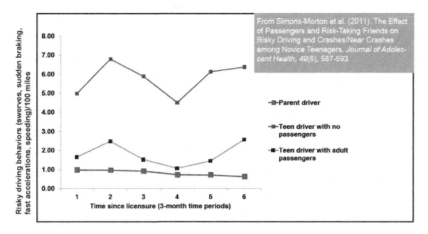

From Simons-Morton et al. (2011). The Effect of Passengers and Risk-Taking Friends on Risky Driving and Crashes/Near Crashes among Novice Teenagers. *Journal of Adolescent Health, 49*(6), 587-593.

Risky driving behaviors (swerves, sudden braking, fast accelerations, speeding)/100 miles

Time since licensure (3-month time periods)

-■-Parent driver

-■-Teen driver with no passengers

-■-Teen driver with adult passengers

When we completed our naturalistic study, we were able to classify the teen drivers as high, moderate, and low risk based on their involvement in crashes and near crashes. We found that the high-risk group remained high risk, the moderate-risk group became low risk over time, and the low-risk group remained low risk the entire time. How do you determine your teen's risk group classification? In reality, some teens are risky by nature, while some are not. It's hard to know which is which. Risk taking is a very complex thing. We have all known teens who tend to be risky. However, there are cases when seemingly low-risk teens have episodes of risky behavior. I have heard numerous stories of the "model child" who had a beer or two at a party and crashed a vehicle going 90 mph, or texted while driving and crossed the center line, or missed a turn in his or her new sports car and rolled several times. In short, there's no magic formula for determining your teen's risk level. At the very least, you should be aware of the warning signs of a high-risk driver, such as being ticketed for moving violations, car damage (even minor), and a car that is always locked even while in the garage.

If you want to know what high-risk teen driving looks like, I have a story to tell you that involves risk at an astronomical level. When I was growing up, I had a friend named Bruce who became a lifelong friend. Bruce was the ultimate gregarious extrovert and the one who was invariably the life of the party. Bruce loved cars, motorcycles, speed, girls, and fun—not a great mixture. One fateful night, he was riding his 400cc dirt bike home from a party with his girlfriend. He was moving at a rapid pace and drew the attention of a local sheriff in a rural community. Bruce knew some dirt trails in the area, so rather than get into trouble, he decided to *run from the law*.

Now, boys and girls, there is an old saying about running from the law to which you should pay attention: "You can't outrun the Motorola," meaning you can't outpace the radio in every police car. Just so you know, radio waves travel at the speed of light, which is faster than the speed of a dirt bike. And there are few things that our good friends in law enforcement hate more than a high-speed chase. These things *never* end well.

Bruce did okay for a while, but he soon slid off of the road on a sharp curve while traveling at more than 70 mph. He narrowly missed some trees that certainly would have been fatal and slid down a hill to a stop, the bike on top of him and the exhaust pipe burning his leg. As the sheriff came over the hill, he witnessed Bruce's girlfriend beating him with her helmet. The officer apparently was in no particular hurry at that point to make an arrest. Fortunately, Bruce had one thing going for him. If you remember our cake analogy, he had one missing ingredient from his cake that surely would have resulted in a fatal crash: he was wearing his signature Stars and Stripes helmet, which saved him from what would have been a serious head injury caused by both the crash and his girlfriend. Amazingly, Bruce avoided extended jail time; he only had to pay hefty fines and forfeit his license. The reason for this leniency is the crash occurred during the 1970s in rural Kentucky and not in 2020 anywhere in the United States.

Believe me when I tell you that I am not trying to glorify Bruce's behavior. He was literally thousands of times at higher risk of dying during this episode than he was for the rest of his driving and riding career. It was just a momentary, very bad decision that teens like Bruce make every day. He lived through the experience, but for every story like this with a happy ending, there are a hundred others that end with someone dead or permanently disabled. Bruce himself would be the first to admonish any of his five daughters or any of his grandkids if they pulled a stunt like that.

After reading a story like this, I'm sure that many of you, especially those who are the parent or guardian of teen drivers, are wondering what you can do to ensure your teen's safety while on the road. Just keep reading ...

Training Your Teen to Drive

As a parent, the first thing you should know when your teens reach driving age is that the car you choose for them can make a significant difference in determining their risk of being in a fatal crash. Just as you should when selecting a car for yourself, you should be looking for the crashworthiness of a vehicle. If families were to put their teen drivers in the newest car they owned instead of the oldest, it is estimated that **the teen fatality rate would drop by one-third nationwide.**

If you want to help your teen driver stay safe, establish firm rules, including no texting while driving.

According to the IIHS, good cars for teens to drive tend to be newer, have electronic stability control and multiple other safety features, and are at least moderate in size and weight (vehicle mass being an important factor in mitigating crash risk). Also, a recent finding from a VTTI/NIH study shows that there is some advantage to *sharing* a car with your kids rather than buying them one of their own. Although the risk is similar for both, shared cars are usually driven less by teens, thus limiting their *exposure* to crash risk in general. In fact, VTTI completed a study with several NIH and Johns Hopkins colleagues and found that **during the first year of licensure, teens with**

primary vehicle access drove five times more miles and were *four times* more likely to get into a crash or near crash compared to teens with shared access to a vehicle.

Just some food for thought. Now, assuming you have selected the best car for your teen that you can afford, what's next?

When you are a novice at something, chances are you will make lots of mistakes. This is true of everything, from basketball to chess to driving. Unfortunately, when it comes to driving, mistakes can have *huge* consequences. Crash rates are the highest when you first get your license, and the rate doesn't change much over the first year of driving. This is true regardless of your age, but the younger the driver, the higher the crash rate. There is a reason that car insurance rates drop for "kids" at age 25: it really takes that long for them to become fully mature, experienced, functioning drivers. Seriously, it takes about six years for the risk for young drivers to drop to the low crash rates of experienced adults! If your kids don't need to learn to drive right away at age 16, talk with them about possibly waiting until they are 17 or 18. If they are not excited about getting a license right away, it's not only okay; it is great! And, chances are, they won't be alone, as there is increasing evidence to suggest that more teens are waiting until they are 18 or older to get a driver's license.

I have to say that two of my most harrowing parental experiences were (1) training my two kids to drive and (2) letting them go once they were licensed. Of course, one might argue that I was anxious because of what I've seen in my profession; after all, I spend all day reading about crashes and such. This may be true, but it's also true that only by doing this work did I become fully aware of the risks my kids would face on the road. Fortunately, this is all behind me now. Congratulations! The fact that you are reading this probably means that you will be in the same boat as I was then! Feel free to call your friends with kids at 2:00 a.m. on prom night; they will be up to console you.

Advice abounds about the "correct" way to teach teens to drive, from the old-fashioned way of riding around with parents for a while to attending very expensive driving and racing schools. Frankly, the results of these schools of thought are pretty mixed. Assuming that the teen spends enough time behind the wheel, all of these methods generally teach teen drivers the fundamentals of how to control a car and interact with traffic. The driver's test

requirement ensures teens can drive at a basic level and understand the rules of the road, for the most part. However, as I've now said many times, the problem is usually not that teen drivers lack knowledge; ultimately, it is their *choosing not to drive safely* that is the biggest safety issue.

I will end this chapter with a few specific tips for effectively training your teens to drive, but before that, I want to offer some more general advice.

What? You Want Me to Sign a Contract?

A fundamental question every parent or guardian needs to answer is, Do you believe driving is a right or a privilege? If you're a teen about to start driving, I know what you're going to say. However, your parents will probably disagree with you. After all, they likely bought the car, pay for the insurance, and are taking a chance that you will keep it together in a dangerous endeavor. Like it or not, this entitles them to set the rules of the house.

When I was 15 and living in Rochester, Minnesota, my home was a couple of miles from the local drive-in theater. That summer my parents allowed me to take the family car to go to the movies with my friends. It was "buck night," which meant that it cost one dollar for a carload to get into the drive-in. What do you think we did? Of course, we piled a dozen kids into my mother's Mercury Monterey—in both the passenger compartment and the trunk—and cruised over to the movies. Sometimes, friends managed to get some beers.

But wait, there's more. Believe it or not, I didn't have a driver's license or even a permit at the time. While my parents (mainly my father) had good intentions by loaning me the family vehicle, this was a recipe for disaster: an overloaded car, no seat belts, underage kids, lots of testosterone, and novice alcohol use. I suppose my dad's logic was that the drive-in was so close to home that nothing truly bad could happen during such a short trip on a lightly traveled rural road. My father was, of course, assuming that we wouldn't drive somewhere else. We made it safely to and from the movies, but my parents were much too trusting in this situation. Our risk level was significantly increased. My point is if you want to help ensure the safety of your teen driver, then you have to set more conservative house rules.

One approach that many parents are taking these days when training their teen drivers is to enter into a contract with them. A contract sets forth the rules and the consequences of violating those rules, and it is imperative that both parties agree to the terms.

Some teen driving contracts employ the concept of "checkpoints." Checkpoints enable young drivers to earn additional independence when certain milestones are reached in good standing. This is based on a concept called "graduated driver's licensing," or GDL. All states have their own GDL laws with respect to newly permitted and licensed drivers. The most accurate statements I can make about these GDL rules are that the stronger rules save a lot of lives and the rules of each state are all over the map (pun intended).

Our friends at the IIHS have developed a handy tool that shows the GDL laws by state and how your teen's crash risk would be lowered if *you* (or your state) enacted more stringent GDL rules. Research has shown that an ideal set of GDL rules includes the following:

1. Issuing a driver's permit on the teen's 16th birthday
2. Receiving 70 hours of supervised driving practice
3. Issuing the driver's license on the teen's 17th birthday
4. Prohibiting unsupervised nighttime driving after 8:00 p.m.
5. Banning teen passengers in the car without supervision until the teen driver is 18

According to the Centers for Disease Control, implementation of GDL programs for 16-year-old drivers could **reduce their fatal crash rate by more than 40 percent;** their overall crash rate would be **reduced by nearly 25 percent.** If all states were to adopt GDL programs, South Dakota would receive the greatest benefit of implementing all of the rules, with a 63 percent reduction in fatal crashes.

Overall, the use of checkpoints has proven to be beneficial. The goal is to keep teen drivers safe and alive. I raised two teens, and I know that telling your kids they can't drive unless they follow these rules is never a pleasant conversation, particularly if their friends don't have to follow the same rules. While certain aspects of the ideal rules may be difficult or even impractical for many families to implement, at least consider enacting them to some degree. The aforementioned IIHS calculator lets you input different levels of different rules to gauge your teen's crash risk, such as no nighttime driving after 10:00 p.m. instead of 8:00 p.m. or having one teen passenger present instead of none. I strongly recommend that you work out a set of rules that keeps your teen as safe as possible while being (mostly) agreeable to all involved. Be strong, and know that your teen will love you again when he or she is 25!

Teens and Alcohol

It's true that the US has an issue with drinking and driving at all ages, but here are some startling statistics about driving and alcohol use in the 16 to 20 age group. Remember, this is the age when there is *zero tolerance* for alcohol while driving a car.

- About 90 percent of college freshmen in the US drink alcohol even though they are (almost) all breaking the law.
- Around 15 percent of 16- to 20-year-old drivers involved in a fatal crash had a BAC above the *adult* legal limit of 0.08 percent.
- About one-half of all fatalities and serious injuries due to alcohol-related crashes happen to passengers, so not riding with an intoxicated driver is just as important as not driving while intoxicated.

To put these statistics into perspective, a few years ago we at VTTI exchanged research on teen driving with some colleagues from Germany. As it so happens, the young driver fatality rate is much lower in Germany than it is in the US, largely thanks to the minimum driving age (18). However, what particularly fascinated us was that our German colleagues felt strongly that we had the alcohol-driving correlation *backwards*. Their opinion was that since the drinking age in Germany is 16 and the driving age is 18, German teens have two years to get used to the effects of alcohol and two years for the novelty of drinking alcohol to wear off before they are able to get behind the wheel.

There may very well be an element of truth in what our German friends were telling us, but there are other safety factors at play. For example, if you are pulled over by police at a traffic stop in Germany (or in a number of other countries), you are required to breathe into the tube to check your BAC or you lose your license for a very long time. If you breathe into the tube and are over the legal BAC limit (0.05 percent in Germany), you also lose your license for a very long time—no muss, no fuss, done deal. This may go a long way toward explaining why people of all ages drink and drive less in Germany, and in many other countries, than they do in the United States.

The lesson to draw from this is that you should never assume your teens won't drink and drive or their friends won't be driving them around after drinking, even at age 16. With this in mind, I have a piece of advice that is purely a personal opinion, and I know it won't sit well with everybody. When my kids were learning to drive, I had to face the possibility that they would find themselves, at one time or another, in a situation involving drinking and driving that left them with few good options. So, I also told my kids—and their friends—that if they needed a ride, at any time of the day or night, for whatever reason, I would pick them up. No questions asked and no punishment of any kind (unless you count my long, arduous lecturing as punishment). All they had to do was call and ask. While my kids were between 16 and 22 years of age, I probably received 10 such calls from them and one or two from their friends. It was well worth the sleep I lost.

Both my kids have continued to take drinking and driving very seriously. They both have pocket Breathalyzers. My daughter has a BAC calculator app on her smartphone. A few years ago, they came to visit and were downtown with several of their friends. They all decided to celebrate a bit and take the local van-ride service that generally charges $5 per person. This night, however, the driver wanted $150 for four of them ("Holidays, freezing rain, bars closed, I can charge what I want"... shame on you!). Anyway, I got "the call" and was very happy to get it. I was tired, it was late and cold out, but it was so much better to get that call than the other call all parents or guardians dread.

Teens and Sleep

Studies have shown that 16- to 18-year-olds need about 8 to 10 hours of sleep each night. Due to circadian rhythm effects, the ideal time for teens to awake is around 8:00 a.m. Of course, for a variety of reasons, teens have to get up earlier to make it to school in many places. Therefore, many teens don't get enough sleep. Why am I telling you this? A 2017 study from the University of Minnesota showed that **a later start time at school reduced teen crashes by about 70 percent.**

Do what you can to make sure your teens are getting a reasonable amount of sleep, especially if they have a long drive to school or work or have a long trip on the horizon.

Trust but Verify

Some of you may remember the old Cold War saying "Trust but Verify," which is why we had treaties enacted while satellites watched our potential enemies. This approach can also be used in teen driving. Essentially, you are in a "Cold War" with your kids, even with a treaty in place, such as the driving contracts described earlier. Even if your teens have gained your trust after a lifetime of teaching them what's right and what's wrong, it is still important to get verification. One method of verification is to form somewhat of a coalition with other parents. We were lucky we lived in a pretty small town with one medium-sized high school. This sometimes resulted in a call or comment from another parent. In other words, there were many sets of eyes in the community. Remember, trust but verify.

Technology is now available that allows parents or guardians to monitor their teens with sensors and even video while the teens drive. In fact, there are many driver monitoring systems on the market today. Some are very simple and measure speed, hard braking, and swerving, while others are quite sophisticated and have cameras. VTTI has developed a research-based monitoring system that is probably the most sophisticated but is currently too expensive to sell. However, I will describe all of its features so that you can get the full picture should you choose (wisely) to go shopping online for an available monitoring system.

The VTTI system, called Driver Coach, is designed to detect all of the riskiest teen driving behaviors, including seat belt use, speeding, swerving, hard braking, fast accelerations, distraction, and fatigue. The detection of alcohol presence will be a future capability of the system. My friend, colleague, and former student Charlie Klauer and I conceptualized an initial study using this system; Andy Petersen and his hardware folks at VTTI built the systems. This system only records video and sensor data when a certain threshold measure has been detected, such as the car traveling faster than 15 mph above the speed limit. If such a threshold is crossed, the system is triggered to record 12 seconds of video and sensor data that are then transmitted to a data reduction center at VTTI. The parents, guardians, and teen participating in the study then receive a report card every week with video clips and the driving behaviors of interest. In essence, the system allows you to *watch* your teen drive, similarly to when you are riding along with the teen. As I have stated before, I have raised two teens and fully understand how excited your kids are going to be about having a system like this in their car. And I fully understand that such systems will mysteriously get broken or stolen from time to time. However, two aspects of these systems may make this option more palatable:

1. The VTTI system, and some other driver monitoring systems, only record data when a threshold value is exceeded. That is, if your teen drives responsibly (no alcohol, no speeding, wearing a seat belt, no aggressive driving, no texting), you will never see anything about his or her driving.
2. VTTI recently installed test systems in the cars of newly permitted drivers. In Virginia this means that teen participants will have these systems in their cars for nine months before they start driving independently. The hope here is that these teen drivers will learn to drive such that the system never collects data, making it agreeable for the teens while teaching them to avoid the highest-risk driving situations.

I recommend that you think seriously about purchasing a driver monitoring system for your teens. If you search the internet for "teen driver monitoring systems," you will see a wide range available. Video is probably very helpful, but those systems are more expensive. Some insurance companies have driver monitoring programs that are fairly low cost. For Driver Coach, VTTI is experimenting with the "calculator model," in which the systems are loaned out for a year from the high school and then returned and reused. In this case the family would only have to pay a small monthly fee (maybe $9.99) for the service. Although not free, this option is cheaper than receiving just one speeding ticket during a year!

A critical point to make here is that if you choose to buy a driver monitoring system, *you have to actively participate in the entire program*. Parents or guardians will reduce their teen's risk if they look at the data provided each week and actively give feedback to their teens. Parents or guardians who do not actively look at data and do not provide feedback will not see much, if any, risk reduction.

Tips for Training Your Teens to Drive

Now, let me conclude with some specific advice for all of you parents and guardians out there who are facing the grim reality of your teens coming of age and getting behind the wheel.

1. **Emphasize that you expect safe, attentive, low-risk driving.** It is your responsibility to teach your teens vehicle-management skills like steering, braking, and obeying the rules of the road. Most importantly, you should emphasize no speeding, no distractions, no alcohol, and no aggressive driving.

2. **Teach them to see, not just look.** My experiences with both of my kids taught me that they would dutifully pull up to a stop sign, look twice both ways, and sometimes pull out in front of a car anyway. Teens don't always fully grasp the concept of sight distance. Not only do they need to be able to see, they need to be able to see far enough, even if they have to creep ahead at the intersection, wait a while to pass a bicycle, or look farther around the curve. In general, you should teach your teens to look as far down the road as they reasonably can and to anticipate what is occurring ahead, in addition to simply keeping the car in the lane. There is nothing handier than seeing the brake lights of a vehicle two cars ahead or the slow-moving truck while you can comfortably change lanes to pass.

3. **Drive around, a lot.** Studies show that the more supervised driving hours teens receive, the better off they are when they become independent drivers. Even though you may be like me—45 hours of driving with my kids seemed like 450—do as much supervised driving with your teen as you can.

4. **Give them the broadest range of driving experiences that you can—and don't be afraid to put them in unusual situations.** Frankly, teens (and any new drivers for that matter) just aren't very good at dealing with the unexpected. So, when it snows, take your teen to the empty shopping center and have them spin out and correct the vehicle. If it's icy, make them practice going slow and steering and stopping in full control; also

make them stop while going downhill (at a safe location so you're not endangering other drivers while practicing). Have your teen drive in the fog and point out that they can't see far enough ahead to stop. Take them as a passenger to a pedestrian area on a Saturday night (college towns are good for this scenario) and let them watch the kids pop out from between cars. Let them drive (for a while; watch for drowsiness symptoms!) on a long trip so they understand what it's like to get tired while driving.

5. **Forget racing school.** Performance racing-type schools are now commonplace, and they all claim great benefits when it comes to teaching driving skills. These schools can teach a higher level of driving skills while making teens more confident in their driving abilities. However, this can also be problematic: regardless of the skills acquired, an overconfident teen driver is a dangerous thing behind the wheel of a car. There's also the fact that these programs are expensive, so if your kids are really determined, they can pay for it themselves when they're adults.

6. **Be calm, patient, and constructive.** I know you've heard this before, but staying calm and patient was the hardest part for me when teaching my kids to drive. Let's face it: it's difficult to remain calm when your kid is about to hit something. But here's the thing. VTTI and the NIH conducted a teen practice driving study involving 90 teen drivers and 131 parents. The study collected data during the entire practice driving period and up to one year following licensure. One important finding was that teen driver errors decreased over time, likely due to improved practice time and parent instruction. Moreover, crash rates during supervised practice driving were low, with no severe crashes occurring. On a side note, the study found that teen driver engagement in secondary tasks increased during supervised driving, suggesting that there is room for improvement in the ways teens receive supervised instruction.

9. Senior Drivers

Rage Against the Dying of the Light

My wife Melissa and I have had two parents who lived long enough that they had to give up driving. My father did so after a series of strokes, while for Melissa's mother the cause was poor eyesight caused by macular degeneration.

I was fortunate to be able to help my father after his strokes because he lived in an assisted living facility close to my house. At that stage he had lost his mobility to the point that he couldn't walk without assistance. The damage caused by his strokes was such that his vision and balance were impaired. Even then, losing his independence was very hard for him. I recall one time when I took him to the local grocery store to do some weekly shopping. As I often did, I parked by the curb at the store, helped him into a motorized shopping cart, and then went to park the car while he waited. Normally, I would then accompany him into the store, helping him get around and find what he needed. This time, however, my father decided to exercise his independence.

As I was parking the car, I saw him look around, and with a wry smile on his face, he took off on his cart and into the store without me. I was worried that I might find him under a pile of soup cans or plowing through an aisle filled with fellow shoppers. After I parked and ran into the store, I found him cruising around in the wine aisle putting bottles in his basket. The bad news for him was that he could no longer drink because of his medications. But he was a good sport as I put the wine bottles back and we continued to shop. I tried to point out the risks involved in what he had done. In the end, though, I couldn't really scold my father, and we had a good laugh about it.

It is *very* hard to give up one's mobility. In essence, the person is losing some degree of independence, even with the growing availability of public transit, rides from family and friends, and the resources to call a cab, Uber, or Lyft when needed. That person can't just hop in his or her own car and go whenever, and wherever, they choose. With this in mind, my mother-in-law, Nancy, told me that no seniors would read this book because it would just tell them they can't drive. I took her comment to heart and decided to approach the subject from a different angle. Specifically, in this chapter I focus on two points:

1. Why older drivers are safer than you think.
2. How we can all maintain our mobility as we grow older.

At VTTI we performed a study several years ago that required younger and older drivers to react to an imminent crash event. We found that, unsurprisingly, the younger drivers had faster reaction times to hitting the brakes. However, the older drivers were able to stop in a slightly shorter distance. You may ask, How is that possible? Well, the younger drivers were quick to get a foot on the brake, but then they hesitated for a brief moment while they decided the best course of action, such as steering instead of, or in addition to, braking. Even though it took them longer to get to the brakes, older drivers hit those brakes hard and without hesitation. Whether this was because of experience or because they knew on some level they needed to compensate or adapt, the older drivers were more effective at making an emergency stop.

From societal and public safety perspectives, there's not an older-driver problem. Seniors (aged 74 plus) are consistently at the *lowest crash risk* of all driving-age groups on a *per licensed driver basis*. One reason for this lowered risk is that older drivers generally adapt very well for a very long time despite growing limitations in vision, cognition, motor skills, reaction time, and physical flexibility.

You may have noticed the term *per licensed driver* in the previous paragraph. Older drivers tend to drive substantially fewer miles than younger age groups do. When you look at the individual skill levels of older drivers, it's more instructive to look at the crash rate *per mile driven*. In that case we see what is known as the "bathtub" curve, with seniors mirroring the high crash rates seen among the youngest and least experienced drivers.

Interestingly, some in my field believe that the higher crash rate per mile traveled for seniors owes largely to the seniors who travel very few miles. Some scholars conjecture that in those few miles senior drivers may travel more hazardous roads or experience more elevated levels of impairment and risk. Of course, at some point drivers who live long enough can no longer adapt. It may be that the older drivers who crash the most can simply no longer compensate by driving on slower and safer roads, in limited traffic, in good weather, in daylight, etc.

On a per licensed driver basis, older drivers have a lower crash risk than other age groups because they tend to adapt well to driving conditions. VTTI conducts studies to help understand the unique risks facing older drivers.

Another point to consider in this discussion is how we as human beings age, both individually and as a population. As we get older, we become more physically fragile, which means the risk of sustaining a serious injury or a fatality is far greater per crash among older drivers compared to younger drivers. Therefore, we need to prevent crashes by using a variety of counter-measures, including making vehicles that aren't just crashworthy but crash-worthy in a way that specifically helps aging drivers and their passengers.

We are an aging society, and such aging of society is projected to continue well into the middle of this century. Whatever issues we see on the road today will be even greater challenges tomorrow. Additionally, those of us of the baby boomer generation, who are creating this "gray tsunami," will likely be fundamentally different from our parents and grandparents regarding a wide variety of factors that may impact driving safety. Those factors may include general health and vigor, driving patterns, living conditions, level and desire for activity, and acceptance of technology, among others.

These changes pose certain challenges with respect to mobility. How do we keep us all mobile? My friend and colleague Jon Antin directs the Center for Vulnerable Road User Safety at VTTI. This center studies younger and older drivers, as well as those who are largely unprotected in the transportation community, such as pedestrians and bicyclists. I asked Jon to help me identify some of the ways we can address the unique needs of older, or more mature, drivers. Here is what we came up with:

1. *Building connected/automated vehicles.* I will discuss this new generation of vehicle technology in chapters 11 and 12, but for now let me just say that these evolving technologies have the potential to significantly help older drivers who can no longer operate vehicles safely on their own. Of course, these systems must be *well-designed* with older drivers in mind.

2. *Creating more "livable communities" and more well-designed shared roadway spaces.* By *livable* I mean communities that emphasize safe and affordable transportation options. Some of this is already under way, such as the efforts to make roads more accommodating to bicyclists and pedestrians. However, we also need to think more about seniors on the road (as both drivers and pedestrians) and incorporate their needs into these efforts.

3. *Training the brain.* We have evidence suggesting that brain exercises can benefit senior drivers. For example, the Advanced Cognitive Training for Independent and Vital Elderly (ACTIVE) trial found brain exercise programs to be effective in improving the cognitive performance of older persons. The results were inconclusive, however, as to which exercises offer the most benefit.

4. *Improving the useful field of view through practice and exercise.* In driving, *useful field of view* is the degree to which you can process relevant information seen in your peripheral vision. Unfortunately, your useful field of view declines with age, and this negatively impacts your driving ability. Measuring the field of view that you can practically use has been the most successful way to predict any meaningful outcomes in real-world driving safety. The good news is that we have evidence suggesting you can improve your useful field of view functionality through

practice and exercise. This may in turn reduce your crash risk and allow you to be mobile longer.

Thus far, you'll notice that I have avoided raising the question of when to quit driving. I've done this for a few reasons. First, there is no formula for determining when someone should stop driving; functional age varies greatly from person to person. Some people in their 90s can drive more safely than other people who are in their 70s. Second, there is a vast amount of information out there to help older drivers gauge their driving ability. For instance, both the American Association of Retired Persons (AARP) and American Automobile Association (AAA) have excellent websites to assist senior drivers. (See References at the end of this book for more information.) Of course, this means that the senior driver needs to be able to use the internet or enlist someone who can. Third, I want Nancy and other senior drivers to read this book because they will find in it useful advice and resources that will make it possible for them to drive safely and thereby extend the time they are able to stay behind the wheel.

10. Motorcycles and a Few Tips for Those Who Ride Them

When I was a junior in high school in Rochester, Minnesota, my father was transferred to Atlanta, Georgia. We had some debate about whether I would come with the family or just stay behind so that I could finish high school in Rochester. I had a girlfriend, friends, etc., and wasn't too excited about starting over in a new school. In the end I moved to Georgia with them. The conditions my father and I agreed upon were that he would give me $1,000 and his motorcycle at the end of the school year and that I could travel anywhere I wanted all summer long. I rode 4,000 miles that summer and spent less time in Minnesota than you might think, because by that time my girlfriend had left me for one of my best friends (sigh). I was 17 at the time and, oddly enough, the thought of riding 4,000 miles on a motorcycle wasn't nearly as crazy sounding as it is today. A lot of my friends had bikes, and we often commuted on bikes to save gas and have fun. A few years of racing dirt bikes made me a pretty safe rider because I always assumed that hitting the pavement would lead to my own death, which was a pretty good assumption.

Riding a sports bike, like this Kawasaki Ninja, significantly increases your crash risk.

As a motorcyclist, I've had some close calls on the road that taught me a lot about principles such as conspicuity, but I never had a crash. Having just wrote this, I must confess that I would never, never, never let my kids do what I did. Why? The answer is simple: motorcyclists have the highest risk of a fatal crash among all transportation users (cars, trucks, etc.):

- **Per mile traveled, motorcyclists are *about 30 times more likely* to die in a crash than those traveling in passenger cars.**
- **If you ride a sports bike (think leaning forward and going fast, such as an Interceptor, Ninja, GSX-R, etc.), you are *more than 100 times more likely* per mile traveled to die in a motorcycle crash than in a car crash.**

This is why some in the driving-safety business don't call them motorcycles; they call them donor-cycles. But hey, we're all adults (or soon will be), and motorcycles are fun. You can make your own decisions, and I might need a kidney someday.

In all seriousness, though, I could write an entire book about how to control and reduce risk on a motorcycle (which might happen if you all like this book). One of the keys to success is experience—sheer time spent on the bike. Of course, this assumes you can survive that long. Training probably helps, particularly programs that are comprehensive and teach defensive riding techniques (look up courses available near you on the Motorcycle Safety Foundation website, listed under References at the end of this book). However, the real biggies in terms of reducing risk are discussed below. To help me with this section, I asked a VTTI motorcycle safety expert, Shane McLaughlin, to weigh in with a few tips. Shane is a friend, former student, and colleague who heads the VTTI Motorcycle Research Group.

Recognize How Bikes Are Different

Very few motorcyclists can brake as hard, or swerve as dramatically, as they can in a car. Just assume for a moment that you are not one of those very few. If you drive a motorcycle the same way you drive a car, you're going to get into trouble. After a crash in a car, the discussion is usually about vehicle insurance, sometimes health insurance. With a similar crash on a motorcycle, the ensuing discussion is more likely to be about disability or life insurance. On a motorcycle, you have to avoid the crash altogether through a series of protective measures.

Know Your Riding Proficiency

Twenty-seven percent of riders involved in fatal crashes do not have a valid motorcycle license. Some of these riders have had their licenses revoked, but others just never bothered to get licensed in the first place. This undoubtedly means that these riders are less proficient in general than those who took the time to learn. Even if you have trained (highly recommended) and have a proper license, each time you get on your motorcycle, think about how long it has been since you last rode. Think about how rusty you are and what might need some work or practice. Consider the extra tasks involved in driving a motorcycle compared to driving a car. For example, if you are looking for traffic as you approach an intersection while on a motorcycle, can you do so while downshifting, balancing, reading signs and signals, and braking smoothly? If it has been a while since you've been on your bike, put in the necessary practice (it makes perfect, after all). If you're riding with friends, pick ones who will accommodate the pace you need to maintain your safety.

Turns Will Get You

A major source of injuries and fatalities for motorcycle riders is going too fast while taking a turn.

A major source of injuries and fatalities for motorcycle riders is going too fast while taking a turn. Keep in mind that you are the only person who has control of your vehicle, so it's critical that you understand the road you are on, read every sign, and maintain awareness of your speed at all times. Think through the layers of protection you have on. Consider how you will manage potential hazards such as sharpness of a turn, gravel or ice in your lane, and limited ability to anticipate oncoming vehicles beyond the curve. When in doubt, always eliminate extra speed before starting to lean so that you are able to avoid any of these hazards.

I Brake for Safety

It's easy enough to gain speed, but how prepared will you be if you need to stop suddenly? Braking can generally get you out of many common crash scenarios. For example, if a line of cars stops in front of you, there's a good chance you will need to brake very hard. So, how good are you at stopping your motorcycle? Part of this goes back to riding proficiency and knowing your bike. You need to allow enough following distance based on your level of riding ability. Arguing about the contribution of the front brake is like arguing about breathing; it's a given that it's a necessity. If you aren't using that brake, you're braking well below the capabilities of the bike.

They Don't See You

We often assume when we drive our car through an intersection that other drivers see us and will obey the traffic laws. More often than not, this is a pretty good assumption to make. Even if you are wrong, you have a lot of steel, plastic, airbags, and seat belts to protect you. None of this is true for a motorcycle. Even though most motorcyclists believe their bikes are easy to see, they are a lot less conspicuous than you might think due to a variety of factors, including the size and profile of the bike, the color of the rider's clothing, and the overall visual contrast with the background environment.

I have two tips for motorcyclists on how to increase your chances of being seen by other drivers:

1. Never assume that other drivers can see you. In fact, assume the opposite—assume that they *don't* see you and that they are about to pull out, change lanes, or otherwise encroach on your space. Always be aware of the closest threats in space and time, and look ahead to determine where you can go if a driver encroaches on your path. In other words, be vigilant, remain suspicious of other drivers, and have an out.
2. Do everything you can to increase your conspicuity. Burn your lights, buy a brightly colored bike, add reflective tape to your bike, buy a kit that flashes your lights, wear reflective clothing, wear light-colored clothing, and buy a brightly colored helmet. You need to actively work at being conspicuous.

Just Because You Can Doesn't Mean You Should, Part 2

If you are a football fan, at one time or another you've probably heard someone say that helmets should be banned from the game. Sound crazy? Not as crazy, my friend, as 31 states getting rid of motorcycle helmet laws or requiring only some riders (usually the younger ones) to wear a helmet. Are you kidding me? If you are ever flying through the air at 60 mph, I'll bet you wish you had one. But hey, just because it is legal doesn't mean that you have to do it, so be a real rebel and wear a helmet—and not just a cereal bowl with a strap on it; wear a real helmet. That way, fellas, your wife/girlfriend/mother/significant other won't have to clean up your drool and wipe your ass (hopefully in that order) for the rest of your miserable life, assuming you even survive a crash without a helmet.

And if that last part sounds sexist, it's because 91 percent of motorcycle fatalities are men; the majority of the other 9 percent are women passengers. Remember what the most dangerous, mind-altering substance is for driving? It's doubly true for riding motorcycles: testosterone! **Wearing a helmet reduces your odds of dying in a crash by almost 40 percent.** That means four more helmeted riders would survive every 10 fatal crashes where no helmet is present.

Natural Selection: Riding Under the Influence

According to our friends at the Motorcycle Safety Foundation, **you are about**

40 *times more likely* (odds = 40.0) to be in a fatal motorcycle crash if you have consumed even a moderate amount of alcohol (BAC greater than 0.05 percent). A BAC of 0.05 percent is not very high. For me, a 185-pound man, it takes only two beers in the first hour to achieve a BAC of 0.05 percent (and only one beer per hour after that). Frankly, though, to ride safely I need to be *well below that limit*—which means no more than one beer, period.

Just to emphasize this point: If I am riding a sports bike while sober, I am already at **100 *times greater risk*** of a crash than if I were behind the wheel of an automobile. That risk ***increases by 40 times*** if I drink a couple of beers. In big round numbers (keeping in mind that calculating your risk is not as simple as exact multiplication), **per mile traveled, you are roughly 4,000 *times more likely* to die in a crash on your sports bike after a couple of drinks compared to driving a car while sober.** Hence the title of this section: riding drunk, particularly on a motorcycle, is just a matter of natural selection.

Are You Really Having a Midlife Crisis?

During the past decade a scary statistic has emerged: fatalities among riders aged 40 and older have increased by 12 percent. **In 2016 more than one-half of fatal motorcycle crashes involved riders over the age of 40.** The older rider group is made up of several different kinds of cats: those who have been riding for a long time, those who are new to riding, and those who used to ride but haven't for a long time. It appears that a lot of these fatal crashes of older riders, or at least the reason for the growth in the fatality rate, fall within the third group, those who haven't been on a ride for a long time but have started riding again. There are probably several factors at play here, including rusty skills, overconfidence, the purchase of a more powerful or bigger bike, and age-related performance degradation. The key here is to ease back into riding. It is important to retrain, consider yourself a novice, and take things slower than you used to ... at least until you've redeveloped your skill level.

Group Riding: Are You the Weakest Link?

If you prefer to ride in a group, you need to keep in mind that there is an increased risk factor at play here relative to the skill level of the least experienced rider in the group. More experienced riders may have the skills necessary to ride faster, take curves faster, stop faster, etc. However, the least experienced riders in the group may be pushing beyond their skill levels to keep up with the group. If you are an experienced rider, be cognizant of various skill levels in your group and don't put your less-experienced buddy in a bad situation. If you are the more inexperienced rider, recognize that other riders may make it look easy. Don't let the moment you run off the road be the time you realize you're not as strong of a rider. Ride within your comfort level; you can catch up a little later.

When riding in a group, keep in mind the difference in skill level among the riders. The least experienced riders may be pushing beyond their skill levels to keep up with the group.

A Special Case of Speed Kills

When I lived in Colorado, I had a four-cylinder Honda 750 ("750 four"). Each year, some friends and I would get together and take a bike trip around the mountains. This, of course, was a lot of fun. During one of these trips, we pulled off at a rest stop to hang out for a bit. After our stop, we were feeling our oats a bit. As we merged back onto the nearly empty interstate, we decided to accelerate to well over 100 mph, something that wasn't hard to do with the bikes we were riding.

As we came over a rise, we saw a state police officer sitting on an overpass. A short time later, we were all pulled over on the side of the road, convinced that we were going to jail. The penalty for going 50 mph or more over the speed limit varies by state, but it is always expensive and never pretty. The officer came up and asked, "Do you know the speed limit?" I said, "Yes, sir, it's 55." He said, "Well, I got you going 70 and your friend here going 75 ..."

We all breathed a huge sigh of relief because we knew he was guessing and didn't get us on radar. But then he said, "Boys, this is your lucky day. I own a Honda CBX 1050 [a six-cylinder bike], and I am sure that you were surprised that you were speeding. So, I am just going to give you a warning this time ... but I will radio ahead, and we will all be keeping an eye on you." The funny thing was that we thought he was just trying to scare us, only to see state patrol cars flash their lights at us twice more that day. It was a good thing we were minding the speed limit. A lucky day indeed.

The message I'm trying to get across here is that motorcycles can be wickedly fast—and our bikes of the past weren't even close to what you can buy today. As a point of comparison, the fastest production car right now, the Bugatti Veyron, can go from 0 to 60 mph in 2.5 seconds. That's damned fast, but not as fast as several motorcycles on the road. As many as seven gas-powered production motorcycles are faster. I say gas powered because, a few years ago, we ran across a new company that makes electric motorcycles called Lightning. A Lightning goes from 0 to 60 mph in 1.5 seconds and has a top speed of 218 mph. (They recommend that you buy it with the fairing or windscreen option if you plan to ride over 180 mph.) There is no production four-wheeled vehicle that can do this. It takes very, very little time to get into trouble on a bike.

Near my house in southwest Virginia, we typically see kids from the nearby college ride along our curvy (meaning fun for them) road on their sports bikes during the spring. When my kids were young and playing near the road, these kids on their sports bikes zoomed by at speeds in the triple digits. It made me want an offensive weapon every now and again. Not only does the road feature sharp curves, but it has suburban neighborhoods, hidden driveways, short sight distances, and slow traffic. As a result, every year one or two sports bike riders on that road end up disabled or dead.

As you might expect, speeding on a bike is a factor in a large percentage of fatal crashes: **33 *percent of motorcycle fatalities* involve speeding, compared to 20 percent for cars and 8 percent for heavy trucks.** Stay at a reasonable speed, no matter how tempting it is to let 'er fly.

11. The Future of Transportation, Part I

Active Safety Systems and Connected Vehicles

We have all seen imaginative depictions of what driving will be like in the future. Just think of the flying cars in *The Jetsons* and *Back to the Future*, or have a look at the 1956 Central Power and Light Company advertisement, shown below, with a car driving itself while a family plays games under a clear glass dome.

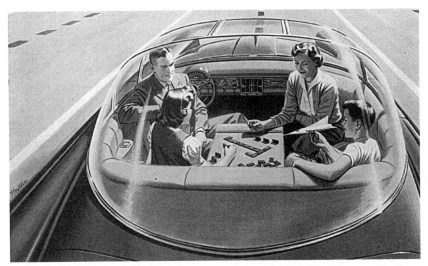

A 1950s vision of the car of the future. The Central Power and Light Company placed this advertisement in leading US newspapers and magazines, including the Saturday Evening Post.

These depictions always have their allure. They imagine a time when traffic jams are a thing of the past and we can be productive or entertained while we commute. And hey, if we can just get rid of all the human drivers, we will all be safe, right? You may be surprised by my answer. But first, I want to talk a bit about the progression of new vehicle technologies.

Active Safety Systems

The cars of today are amazing feats of engineering. Take, for instance, the recent development of *active* safety systems. We've had *passive* safety systems in our automobiles for a long time—seat belts, airbags, crumple zones, etc.—and they are good at increasing your chances of surviving a crash. Active safety systems, on the other hand, help you *avoid* a crash.

In 1991 I helped conduct the first on-road evaluation of an active safety system concept known as forward collision warning (FCW). One of my students at the time was Dan McGehee, now at the University of Iowa, and together Dan and I instrumented a prototype Cadillac with a $15,000 scanning laser from a jet fighter; this laser served as the warning sensor. (Today, automotive radars sell for just a few hundred dollars and are much more capable.)

The study was conducted on-road with a participant who was a novice to the scenario. This person was put behind the wheel of the Cadillac and told to follow another car in front. The driver was told that the lead car was also testing a "variety of advanced technologies," but in reality it was just leading the route and braking at different levels and speeds so we could see how our participant driver reacted. Afterwards we published an award-winning paper (kind of a big deal for academics) in which we pointed to the benefits of this type of active system while providing much-needed information on proper following distance and brake reaction time.

My friend and colleague Rich Deering spent many years at General Motors (GM) doing safety research and design work for safety systems, including the early work on active safety systems. Suppliers and inventors would talk to Rich on a regular basis, trying to sell their active safety ideas to a very large vehicle manufacturer and get wealthy in the process by selling hundreds of thousands of units. Rich used to say on a pretty regular basis that he had a good week because he knew how to solve more than 100 percent of the crash problem. You might wonder how this could be true. Well, it wasn't. But the claims of the inventors and suppliers ("This will reduce rear-end crashes by 50 percent," or "That will reduce run-off-road crashes by 70 percent") added up to more than was even possible. The lesson here, which I will discuss in detail later, is to consider the source when you hear people making amazing claims, especially those about new technology. Treat grand claims with suspicion, and consider the source they come from.

With this warning in mind, let me offer some friendly advice about how to make the most of active safety systems.

Become One with Your Ride

Active safety systems are designed to reduce, and ideally eliminate, the risk of crashing. They employ a variety of technologies to warn drivers of pending danger or to even prevent that danger. For instance, electronic stability control (ESC) automatically controls the power, braking, and wheel slip of each wheel independently. By performing these maneuvers at a high rate of speed, the system can stabilize a car that is sliding or otherwise losing traction. Forward collision warning is another example of an active safety system; it's designed to prevent collision with an object in front of the car (say, another vehicle, a wall, or an animal on the road). Some forward collision warning systems simply alert drivers to the danger while others automatically brake at the onset of a forward collision scenario. A variation on this is automatic emergency braking (AEB), which provides a last-ditch automatic full brake application if a driver fails to respond.

The results are still preliminary as to how effective active safety systems are at reducing injurious crashes. However, our friends at the IIHS tell us the following:

1. Electronic stability control is very effective and **reduces fatal crashes by about one-half** compared to non-equipped cars.
2. Forward collision warnings **can cut rear-end crashes by as much as 23 percent**, but the results vary by manufacturer. Systems that automatically brake, rather than just warn the driver, seem to be more effective (see point number 3).
3. Automatic emergency braking may **reduce injury claims by up to 35 percent.**
4. Lane departure warning systems **may reduce injurious crashes by 21 percent**, but once again, results vary by manufacturer.
5. Blind spot monitoring or detection can **reduce the rate of injurious lane-change crashes by 23 percent.**

It's still too early to produce hard stats, but early results suggest that the effects of these active safety systems may increase when the systems combine with each other. For example, adaptive cruise control appears to be beneficial, especially when paired with forward collision warning and automatic emergency braking. However, these systems *must be well designed*, so look to resources like IIHS to learn about the effectiveness of particular active safety systems.

Active safety systems are continually evolving and will no doubt improve with each model year. However, one thing is certain regarding active safety technology: you need to understand how the system works and what it is telling you. In the past you might have been able to drive away from the dealership in a new car without pausing to read the owner's manual or learn about the vehicle's safety features. Newer technologies, however, require that you take time to learn the active safety features before putting too many miles on the car.

We all know that pretty much *no one* reads the owner's manual of a vehicle, but a number of studies have shown that safety systems can become ineffective or even detrimental if they aren't used properly. This happens when the driver has an incorrect *mental model* of how a system works. In fact, our friends at AAA recently found that more than three-quarters of drivers were unaware of the limitations of their active safety systems or had an incorrect understanding of what the system detected and how it responded. Some, for instance, thought their blind spot monitoring systems detected speeding vehicles or vulnerable road users when in fact they did no such thing. If you're driving a vehicle equipped with ABS, the old standard of "pumping the brakes" won't be necessary.

My friend and colleague at VTTI Eddy Llaneras has conducted dozens of studies of active safety systems. One of these studies focused on a system available in new cars that alerts drivers to objects in their path as they back up. In it he found that some drivers effectively ignored backup warnings (and even automated brakes) as they were backing toward an obstacle behind them. They would look around and, not seeing anything obstructing their path, continue to back up into the object. The problem was that they weren't able to see small objects behind their vehicles. The system correctly detected the obstacle and warned the driver, but the driver backed over the object anyway, trusting their eyes over the warnings. The solution to this problem was to suggest that a backup camera be integrated into the warning system, a configuration that is now a common feature in many newer vehicle models. This is certainly an improvement, but as is often the case with new vehicle technologies, a rear-vision system is only effective if drivers actually use the system—and use it **properly**.

VTTI *regularly tests new vehicle technologies (left) for manufacturers, suppliers, and government agencies on its Smart Roads in southwest Virginia (right).*

Be Aware of Unintended Consequences

VTTI regularly tests new vehicle technologies for manufacturers and their suppliers, even at times for government agencies. Vehicle safety systems go through extensive testing during development, but our testing is designed specifically to put these systems through the rigors of the real world. A big part of what we are looking for are *unintended consequences*—unanticipated results that arise when people use these systems in the real world.

As an example, a few years ago a truck manufacturer built a system that alerted drivers when they were about to cross a lane line on the highway. The manufacturer was marketing the system as a solution to the problem of truckers falling asleep behind the wheel. The idea was that drivers would use the system as a prompt to pull off the road and rest. However, the manufacturer found during the first field tests that drivers were using the system not as a prompt to pull off the road but as an "alarm clock" to wake them when they were tired and falling asleep. In other words, rather than thank their lucky stars and pull over to get some rest, they saw it as a way to continue driving so that they could clock more mileage than before.

In this case the unintended consequence was that drivers were relying on the system to wake them up at the first sign of trouble when, in fact, the manufacturer's intent in designing the system was to prevent trucks from crossing a lane line. The system did nothing to warn drivers of objects ahead (it was never designed to do this), and occasionally the system would "miss" an alert. This overreliance on the system could have actually *increased* crashes rather than reduce them. Fortunately, the system was never deployed in such a configuration.

I bring this up because, as a driver, you always need to be aware of your own behavior behind the wheel and how that behavior affects your use of an active safety system. It's not enough to understand how a particular system works. It's important to use the system as it was intended to be used and not rely on it to do something it was never designed to do.

The Next Big Thing: Cars That Talk to Each Other and Everything Else

Modern cars are essentially rolling computers. Thanks to GPS, they often know where they are, where they are going, and at what speed. Positions measured by an automotive GPS are not terribly accurate, though, with errors as great as 30 feet relative to the car's absolute position on the ground. However, if two cars were to travel close together and talk to the same GPS satellites, their positions *relative to one another* would be pretty accurate. Essentially, if you could make cars that "talk" to each other, they could avoid hitting each other or at least send warnings about impending collisions.

This concept is already a reality—it's called connected-vehicle communication, and it enables vehicles to talk to each other, to the roadside, and to devices such as smartphones. This type of communication uses dedicated short-range radios (essentially a version of Wi-Fi), cellular communications, or cellular communications that act like Wi-Fi. In the latter case, the signal travels from one car directly to another car or a point along the highway instead of through a cell tower. Connected-vehicle communications have huge potential. While using it your car can instantly sense when the car in front of you slams on its brakes. It can just as easily sense when the vehicle five cars ahead of you slams on its brakes.

Connected-vehicle communications can also tell you when you are about to change lanes and hit another car or when you should slow down due to hazardous road conditions. With roadside radios and even radios embedded in cell phones, connected-vehicle communications can tell you when you are about to run a stoplight, when another car is about to run a stoplight, when there is a motorcycle in your blind spot (more conspicuity!), or when you are on a collision path with a bicycle, scooter, or pedestrian. The safety possibilities when using connected-vehicle communications are vast. And perhaps the best part is that you get all of these safety benefits for the cost of a relatively inexpensive radio or cellular device, compared to the more expensive radar, lidar (laser), sonar, and machine-vision (that is, camera-based) sensors.

VTTI has been working with connected-vehicle technology for more than a decade. Much of this work is done through our Center for Advanced Automotive Research, which is directed by Zac Doerzaph. Zac and his group have done a number of studies that show the potential of this technology. It's estimated by our friends at NHTSA that **connected-vehicle technology has the potential to *eliminate about 70 percent of crashes* involving alert drivers.** This is why NHTSA has been working with car companies and suppliers for a long time in determining the next steps forward in connected-vehicle technology. In 2017 the agency issued a Notice of Proposed Rulemaking—essentially, a public notice—to gather feedback about the possible implementation of connected-vehicle technology in vehicles. To date, no mandate has been issued by NHTSA, but it remains a top priority for the agency.

12. The Future of Transportation, Part II

Automated Vehicles

I believe that in my lifetime—or at least in yours if you're younger than I am—we will see automation in vehicles advance to the point where cars will more or less drive themselves. First, though, some concrete realities need to be addressed in the deployment of these vehicles.

A Transportation Revolution?

Tom speaks about the future of transportation at a TEDx Salon talk in Wilmington, Delaware, 2017
(Source: TedX Salon)

In 2017 I gave a TEDx Salon talk in Wilmington, Delaware, about this very subject. One of my main points had to do with common perceptions of automated and autonomous vehicles. Most people think of them as a new development in transportation or as a *revolution* that is about to transform our vehicles and our roadways. This perception is not surprising, given what we overwhelmingly hear in the media. In reality, these systems are not as new as people think. The technology has been gradually developing over the past few decades. Therefore, instead of talking about a transportation revolution, we really should be thinking of it as an *evolution*.

To understand this evolution, it may first help to understand what I mean when I use the terms *automated* and *autonomous*. The Society for Automotive Engineers (SAE) International, which provides information about vehicles and vehicular systems to the public, created a system to classify what they dub "driving automation." It created this system—or taxonomy—because not all advanced vehicles have the same level of functionality. SAE frequently updates these classifications (which in and of itself speaks to an evolution of the technology). The most recent update came in 2018.

The SAE system of classification (SAE standard J3016_201806) divides driving automation into six levels:

- **Level 0—No driving automation.** The driver performs all of the tasks of driving, even when using active safety systems.
- **Level 1—Driver assistance.** The driver performs most of the driving tasks, with limited automated system control of either the steering or acceleration/braking tasks.
- **Level 2—Partial driving automation.** The driver is still responsible for the overall driving task, with the automated system having limited control of both steering and acceleration/braking tasks; for a point of reference, this is generally the level at which the Tesla Autopilot performs.
- **Level 3—Conditional driving automation.** The automated system performs some driving tasks, but the driver is the "fallback" system while the automated system is engaged.
- **Level 4—High driving automation.** The driver is still present in the vehicle, but the automated system performs the entire driving task; there is no expectation for a user to respond to a request to intervene if the automated system is engaged.
- **Level 5—Full driving automation.** The automated system fully operates the vehicle while engaged and the driver is present in the vehicle; there is no expectation for a user to respond to a request to intervene if the automated system is engaged.

The Tesla Autopilot is one example of a Level 2 automated vehicle.

These are very simplistic explanations of the SAE levels of driving automation. If you look at the list, you can see why we differentiate between automated and autonomous driving. With automated driving, the driver still has a role (Levels 1 and 2 and sometimes Levels 3 and 4). With autonomous driving, the driver has no role (Levels 3 and 4 sometimes, Level 5 all of the time). If you want to get ultra-technical, the fact of the matter is that *automated* and *autonomous* are not SAE-approved terms, but exact terminology doesn't really matter to most of us who have to drive (or ride) in these things. The important point is that not all advanced vehicles are the same nor do they require the same level of driver involvement.

Just as there are different levels of driving automation, there are also different applications for automation. Some automated vehicles are meant primarily for individual drivers who use them for personal needs. Think of Tesla as an example. Then there are rideshare and on-demand vehicle programs that have various service-based revenue models not dependent on individual vehicle purchases. For example, Book by Cadillac and Maven Reserve let drivers in larger US cities rent Cadillac or Chevy vehicles for a flat fee. These on-demand vehicle programs have options with limited automated features at this time, with the opportunity to feature more automation as such vehicles become available.

Other automated vehicles that you may see soon are robotic taxis. It is likely that these vehicles will initially be "last-mile" applications—applications that help people travel the last leg to their final destination—as part of a larger transit system along a single (sometimes dedicated) corridor and will gradually grow to include more urban corridors and other types of commutes. It's difficult to predict how this part of the automation picture will unfold. However, it's safe to say that it will be many years before such services are provided ubiquitously in both urban and rural areas (just think of the amount of time, space, and bureaucratic red tape we would have to weed through to build a dedicated corridor).

Another application of driving automation is truck platooning. The concept behind truck platooning is increasing fleet efficiency, fuel economy, and safety by grouping semitrucks together such that they travel in a "pack" using connected-vehicle communications and automated lane keeping and cruise control. In these platoons, only the lead truck would have an active driver, while the remaining trucks would have either no driver or a driver that could sleep or do other tasks. However, there are complexities to truck platooning, such as the inevitable car that tries to cut in front of a group of trucks because the car driver is trying to make an exit, pass someone, etc. Our researchers at VTTI are currently studying these situations to determine if there is an ideal distance between trucks that discourages car cut-ins. Remember, trucks are bigger and have more mass than a car, so they can't brake—even automatically—as quickly as a passenger vehicle. One added complexity is the fact that if the lead driver in a platoon fails to drive safely, the result could be five 40-ton vehicles mowing into a line of stopped cars on the interstate or going through the guardrail into a suburban neighborhood. In other words, despite all of the advantages, these platooning systems need to be close to perfect when they hit the road.

What's It Really Like Being in an Automated Vehicle?

One of the more fun and interesting parts of what we do at VTTI is driving the latest and greatest production (and sometimes prototype) cars when they first come out. For instance, we have been able to drive a number of cars with some level of automated control in the lateral (steering) and longitudinal (accelerating and braking) dimensions (think SAE Level 2 or Level 3 driving automation). At this time there are about six cars out there with these features, although all are different in design. At this point, most of them are designed primarily for open highway use and almost all of them expect you to keep your hands on the steering wheel and pay attention as you would in a car with no such features.

At VTTI we've conducted a number of studies designed to tell us what drivers might actually do in these cars as opposed to what the manufacturer or dealer tells them to do. Surprise! The two often don't match. This is why looking for unintended consequences is so important when we are evaluating new advanced-vehicle technology. Drivers don't always use a system as intended, so we need to know what happens in such instances. Better to find out *before* the system is widely used than afterwards.

I was driving one of these new automated-vehicle models recently. In doing so, I assumed the role of a driver who was inexperienced with the vehicle—a driver who probably didn't fully read and understand the owner's manual (about 90 percent of us are guilty of this) or didn't pay attention to the dealer when picking up a $120,000 car full of exciting features that the driver just wanted to get out on the road (probably what at least 99 percent of us would do).

I set the system on automated control on an interstate near my house and proceeded to test its limits. I am a safety professional, so don't try this at home. I took my hands off the wheel and headed on a three-hour trip to one of VTTI's other testing facilities. The car did pretty well, reminding me occasionally to put my hands back on the steering wheel, which I did for a second or two before continuing hands-free. This model of car changes lanes by itself when the turn signal is activated, so I was passing cars in pretty heavy traffic. Then, it started to rain, which generated some splash and spray from an adjacent semitruck. For some reason, the car decided to steer hard left toward the guardrail. My hand was right near the wheel, so I was able to recover control quickly. In another second, though, I would have had a different story to tell. Lesson learned. The automation system didn't work well in a low-visibility circumstance. This shortcoming is understandable, but it's a problem that requires a warning and subsequent transfer of control back to manual driving.

As I continued on my trip, the weather cleared and traffic subsided, which made me think, "Hey, now is a good time to use the system in conditions where it should work well." And it did work well ... most of the time. During my trip the car would have left the road probably two to three more times had I not manually intervened to prevent it. Again, that's fine *as long as the driver's hands are on the wheel and he or she is paying attention.* However, the danger is that drivers will adapt to automated systems in such a way that they rely on it too much, allowing themselves to take their eyes off the road for too long. They might also become sleepy because they have nothing to do or the scenery is boring—both of which are unintended consequences of this technology.

Researchers in our VTTI Center for Automated Vehicle Systems recently studied how drivers respond to Level 2 and Level 3 automated vehicles. The results suggest that drivers of automated cars respond more slowly to prompts the longer they are in the car. Some participants ignored alerts while engaging in a secondary task, which tells us that some users are likely to treat driving as the secondary task, a behavior that will have its own set of unintended consequences.

To explain what I mean, I want to return to Gene Farber, who I mentioned earlier in the book. Gene was a driving-safety engineer at Ford for many years, and he influenced a lot of folks in our field, including me. The main reason for his influence was that he was a principled pragmatist who valued science that could be applied in whatever form to save lives, including in car design, driver education, and coherent safety laws. But another reason is that Gene was a great "BS detector"—something that is extremely valuable in our business. Everyone knows how to solve the driving safety problem, but most of the so-called solutions don't work. Gene knew when someone was playing the BS card. He also had a great sense of humor, which meant that he knew how to call it out in entertaining ways.

One time Gene and I were listening to a presentation about an automated vehicle in development that could drive itself under most conditions and most of the time. The driver could essentially rely on the car to steer, maintain speed, and brake if needed. The driver's sole task was to be alert and watch in case something unusual happened, at which time the driver would need to take control back from the vehicle. At the end of the talk, Gene observed, in his own unique and acerbic way, "Are you crazy? The driver won't be ready to take control because they'll be having sex in the back seat."

Gene's point was that humans are basically terrible at staying alert and watching for something that rarely happens. It's a lesson we learned (or should have learned) many years ago from the nuclear power industry–think of Three Mile Island. We will soon be seeing vehicles on the road in large numbers with systems that have sensors to monitor the state of the driver. These systems are amazing, but the danger is that we will become so dependent on them that we will fail to be ready when something goes wrong, which it inevitably will at one time or another.

The best way to be ready for such situations is to take time to understand how these advanced systems work. Whenever you are driving a car that has some type of new automated feature–like automated emergency braking or lane keep assist–you need to know how the system works, when it works, and when it doesn't work. Therefore, it's best to start out driving *as though the system doesn't exist.* The way these systems are currently being designed, they are basically intended to be a backup if the driver fails–in other words, if *you* fail. It's very important you realize that you are still in charge and that you must be ready at all times to be the beast of a crash-avoiding driver that you are, which no automated system can readily replace. By driving this way, the automated systems help you be safer by acting as a redundant safety system–similar to my wife, who currently serves this purpose by faithfully yelling at me whenever I do something wrong while driving. A redundant system is effective because *both* the driver and system have to fail in order to crash.

We've seen in VTTI studies how drivers may adapt to automated systems in unsafe ways. My friend and colleague, Naomi Dunn, and I recently completed a study for our friends at the AAA Foundation for Traffic Safety. We found that people behave differently with automation depending on several factors, namely: 1) how much they had used it and 2) whether the automated car was theirs or borrowed. For new users, there was a "novelty" phase where they "tested" the systems while they were learning. This involved purposely ignoring the system if it asked the driver to take control, or otherwise determining the system's limits–like testing automated braking by *not* braking to see if the car would really brake by itself. This is not something we recommend doing, for the obvious reason that if you test the system without really knowing how it works, the test itself can get you into a crash! Instead, it is better to be that completely redundant safety system that you are and learn and follow all of the instructions and recommendations for advanced vehicle systems.

Another phenomenon occurred in this same study, after drivers had driven with the automated systems for a few months (the post-novelty phase). What we saw here was that drivers started to trust the systems too much on occasion, or they overly adapted to the additional automated capabilities (think steering and braking) afforded by the systems. This adaptation included taking their eyes off the road for longer periods (remember the most important point in this book relative to reducing your crash risk: *keep your eyes on the road!*). This all supports the points made earlier about advanced-vehicle technology: working *with* the technology in your car the way it was designed to be used is critically important, and adapting by adopting bad behaviors can always increase your risk, even with highly sophisticated systems.

Human Drivers Are Really, Really Good ... for the Most Part

As I've tried to show, automated cars and trucks are not perfect, and they will not be perfect for some time. This will change someday, but the pace of change will be slower than most people think. However, if you talk to some advocates today, you might come away with the impression that automated-vehicle technology is already perfect or near perfect. These advocates will point out that more than 37,000 people die annually on US roadways, with 94 percent of those fatalities due to human error. Therefore, they argue that deploying this technology immediately can do no more damage than human drivers. There is some validity to this argument, but it's also too simplistic. For instance, it doesn't account for contingencies such as what happens if fatalities occur at the fault of automated vehicles. Will people be as willing to jump into these vehicles when they hear crash stories from their friends or read about them on the internet? In such cases, it won't matter that the number of fatalities is actually much lower than the number caused by human drivers.

It also must be said that human drivers aren't that terrible. To return to my friend Gene (the BS detector), he once developed a driving behavior model that revealed that an average US driver will make approximately 3,000,000 successful braking maneuvers *with one failure* (a rear-end crash) during 25 years of driving. The drivers will successfully brake in all kinds of weather and lighting conditions, in numerous odd and anomalous scenarios, despite other drivers doing strange things around them.

Early in my career I worked at the University of Iowa with high-fidelity driving simulators. These simulators allowed us to create any number of traffic scenarios, no matter how unlikely. In one case we were trying to determine whether a radar-based forward crash avoidance system would be beneficial in helping distracted drivers avoid crashes. So, we distracted the driver and created a "reveal" scenario during which a simulated lead truck would suddenly swerve out of the lane, revealing a stationary car in the driver's lane. Based on everything we knew about driver performance, such as reaction time, we calculated that at least one-half of the drivers could not possibly avoid the crash. After running 50 or more drivers through the scenario, *nobody crashed.* They avoided hitting the stopped vehicle by a number of methods, including swerving to the shoulder and not braking, slowing down to let a vehicle pass in the adjacent lane and then swerving left, and just hitting the brakes faster than expected.

Woman using a driving simulator that recreates the experience of driving under the influence of alcohol. She is wearing glasses that distort her vision.

By contrast, our research at VTTI shows that drivers in automated cars can't be relied on to monitor and react like they can in manual driving. Even if they're not having sex in the back seat, drivers will read, write, and do many other things while the car drives itself. My friend Eddy Llaneras and other colleagues have shown that drivers take their eyes off the road for as much as 30 *seconds in even partially automated driving.* To put that into perspective, it takes a little more than three seconds to travel the length of a football field at highway speeds. Taking your eyes off the road for 30 seconds is, well, being completely disengaged.

The average driver in the US has, overall, one serious, police-reported crash every 17.9 years of driving. A good driver who chooses to drive alert, attentive, and sober reduces that risk by a factor of three. This means that a large portion of the US population will go through their lifetimes *never* experiencing a serious crash. To match this, automated vehicles need to be damn near perfect when they are deployed.

But Nothing Is Perfect, so When Will Automated Vehicles Be Here?

By my estimate, it will take us another two years or so, at the very least, before we see *nearly perfect* automated vehicles in limited use. That's 2022, if we're being optimistic. I say this based on the fact that we've been testing automated-vehicle technology for a long time at VTTI, and we know that the deployment of advanced technology takes a while. Earlier I told a story about testing forward collision warning systems back in the 1990s. It's taken more than 20 years for such systems to be integrated into newer vehicle models, and we're still not at 100 percent deployment. The same is true for automated emergency braking (AEB), which became available for the first time in the US in 2013. AEB means that if your car senses you are going to crash and that you are not responding, it will brake (very hard) for you. This technology is accepted by everyone now, with 20 car manufacturers volunteering to get it on their vehicles by 2022. Yet, we were testing AEB at VTTI more than 20 years ago. To put it into perspective, the chart below from IIHS illustrates the time expected to deploy AEB on a widespread basis.

Drivers can expect a mixed fleet of autonomous and conventional cars for decades. Autobrake, for example, won't be in 80 percent of registered vehicles until 2033, even with automakers' pledge to make it standard by 2022.

Predicted penetration of autobrake into vehicle fleet

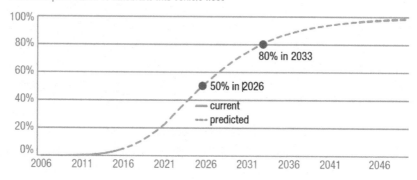

A realistic timeline of deploying advanced-vehicle technology. Source: IIHS

I point this out because 20 or so years is the standard amount of time it takes to deploy new technology and get it through a transportation fleet. That is the fastest rate of progress.

If we use the IIHS chart to illustrate the general trajectory of automated technology deployment, it should take 13 years from the time the technology is *nearly perfected* for about 50 percent of vehicles to have substantial automation. That's only 50 percent deployment by the year 2035—and we're assuming that nothing else goes wrong. It will take roughly twice that amount of time (27 years, or the year 2049) before we reach the point that 90 percent of vehicles on the road have substantial automation. And this is just an estimate. Automated-vehicle technology may not be deployed this fast for any number of reasons, including the public's willingness to accept and adopt driving automation.

Automated Vehicles and You: What's Your Risk Perception?

When will be the right time for you to purchase or ride in a car that drives itself? The answer depends on how much risk you're willing to take, or your "risk perception." *Risk perception* means that there is an actual risk associated with doing something and, depending on the individual, there are differing levels of *perception* of that risk. People are sometimes terrible at judging actual risk. Just think about commercial airlines. Many people realize that flying commercially is safer than driving a car, but they generally don't have an accurate sense of how much safer it really is. If you were to conduct a survey, most people would say that flying is twice as safe as driving, but if you look at fatalities over the years, it's really 2,000 times more safe to fly as it is to drive. The perception of risk is drastically different than actual risk.

Two factors will largely determine the public's perception of risk with respect to automated vehicles. The first is "dread risk," which speaks to one's ability to visualize a scary outcome. For example, literally 100 people die every day on our roadways, but people don't view driving as that risky. For some reason, they don't imagine themselves in a car crash, thus manual driving gets a bye. Let's compare that risk to, say, shark attacks. When a shark attack occurs in the US, it is a tragic event, people get off the beach, and it's in the mainstream media for days. It seems that people have no problem imagining themselves being bitten by sharks. Yet, the reality is that we kill more people on roads *in one day* than sharks have killed *in the last 200 years in US waters.*

The second factor in determining people's risk perception is the degree to which they feel that they have control over a situation. For drivers of automated vehicles, that risk is perceived relative to the control they have in manual driving. This perception gets us into the concept of the risk-benefit ratio. When drivers are eventually put in a situation in which they have no control (e.g., fully autonomous driving), their perception of equal risk to manual driving (i.e., drivers in total control) will be up to 1,000 times lower (think commercial airline safety).

What will the risk perception be when it comes to automated vehicles? If we assume that the perceived risk will be 1,000 times greater for autonomous vehicles when compared to manually driven vehicles–and considering that approximately 37,000 people die on US roads each year–this means that only 37 *fatalities* can occur each year in autonomous vehicles for them to be perceived as safe as manual vehicles.

These are tough odds for automated vehicles to beat, made even tougher by a few other factors. An important component of risk perception will be how automated-vehicle-related crashes are treated in the media. For instance, when a fatal crash involving the Tesla Autopilot happened in 2016, nearly 250 national media outlets covered the story. Yet, when a similar manual crash occurred—that is, the driver crashed into the side of a semitruck at an intersection, resulting in one occupant death—less than five media outlets covered the story, none of which were national news outlets.

Within a span of about a week in early 2018, Uber and Tesla made national news due to fatalities involving their automated vehicles. The Uber crash, which occurred in Arizona, was the first known fatality involving a pedestrian and an automated vehicle, in this case a Volvo XC90 SUV that was operating in autonomous mode with a test driver behind the wheel. The 2018 Tesla crash involved a driver operating a Tesla Model X in Autopilot mode that crashed into a highway barrier in California. In both cases we saw immediate media reactions, most questioning whether automated vehicles could really operate ubiquitously and safely (not to mention questions of data use, technology updates, driver responsibility versus manufacturer/supplier responsibility, liability, etc.). As a result, Uber pulled its automated-vehicle testing in Arizona, while Tesla continued to assert that, relatively speaking, automated-vehicle technology will still be safer than manual driving.

It is still unclear if the public agrees with Tesla. A January 2018 Reuters poll of more than 2,500 adults found that two-thirds weren't too comfortable with the idea of being in an autonomous vehicle. An overwhelming majority had more faith in humans than autonomous systems when it came to driving. Add to this the fact that manually driven vehicles continue to sell at a brisk pace and you start to develop a better picture of the realities of interest in autonomous vehicles.

The Good, Bad, and Unpredictable: Autonomous Cars Will Always Have to Deal with Drivers

There are still other factors to consider when you talk about large-scale automated-vehicle deployment. (I hope by this point you're starting to see how complex this issue really is.) A big issue for designers of these systems is that for decades to come—and probably forever—there will always be human drivers on the road to contend with. Why? The history of driving tells us that when new technologies are introduced, driver compliance is never 100 percent. Let's look at a few examples:

- **Seat belts.** Despite the ubiquity of seat belts and the fact that people know they save lives, 10 to 20 percent of people still do not wear seat belts.
- **Drunk driving.** Despite numerous campaigns and educational outreach initiatives, 12 percent of drivers in the US admit to driving while intoxicated.
- **Automatic transmission.** The automatic transmission was invented more than 70 years ago, but even today 5 percent of vehicles on the road have manual transmission, even though manual is generally more expensive than automatic.

Another factor to bear in mind is that driving or riding in automated vehicles can cause motion sickness. Our friends at the University of Michigan Transportation Research Institute (UMTRI) found that about 12 percent of US adults riding in self-driving cars will experience motion sickness at some point. This actually makes a lot of sense, given that motion sickness is generally due to a lack of control over individual motion.

We also can't dismiss the fact that some people just like to drive. There are performance and sports car enthusiasts out there who are not proponents of automated driving. If you spend any time watching *The Grand Tour* on Amazon (or its predecessor, *Top Gear*, on BBC), then you've likely seen an entire crowd of gearheads jeer at the mere mention of automated vehicles.

How does all of this affect the transportation system? In a utopian world we would have perfect automated vehicles at 100 percent deployment, with all of them following the same rules across the board. But this is a fantasy. Manual driving will *always* be around, and there will always be manual drivers who do not follow the rules, just as many manual drivers don't follow the rules today. Case in point: the average speed on US interstates is *greater than the posted speed limit*. This means that more than 50 percent of drivers are violating the law every day. Another example comes by way of Zac Doerzaph, whose study of intersection behavior (mentioned earlier) found that less than 50 percent of drivers came to a full stop at a stop sign. Maybe that's not entirely surprising, but one stat from Zac's study should raise some eyebrows: the average speed for those who did not stop was 11 mph; some people were up to 20 mph. The point is that automated vehicles will have to operate in a world with manual driving, and it's very difficult for automated-vehicle technology to develop the intelligence to predict highly variable, and rule-breaking, human behavior.

Yes, automated-vehicle deployment is happening on a small scale. You can drive hands-off and feet-off in about six production vehicles. However, the levels of autonomy (i.e., SAE Levels 3, 4, and 5) that allow the driver to safely disengage from the driving task altogether do not yet exist anywhere in the world. That's right folks; all of those articles that you read about this automated small bus or taxi all have a safety driver or monitor of some sort. But to circle back to the beginning of this section, deployment of *nearly perfect* autonomous-vehicle systems will happen no sooner than two years from now. If you add 13 years for 50 percent market penetration, we'll be at 2035. By then you'll have experienced a lot of automated-vehicle technology, such as robotic taxis and highway driving. To get to 90 percent market penetration, we have to look ahead to 2049.

Among the automated vehicles you may see soon on the road are robotic taxis, like this one in Las Vegas.

However (I can't emphasize this enough), if the automated-vehicle technology isn't correct from the start, you can add 5 to 10 years to those numbers. If they crash—and crash more than is deemed acceptable—governments and drivers won't accept the technology. They will slow it down because they won't buy it, or legislation will have to be passed to protect the public. This could put us up to 2054 or 2059 for 90 percent market penetration.

No matter the timeline, it is imperative that we continue to pay attention to what is happening on our roadways now. Fatal crashes are on the rise in the US for reasons that are entirely fixable: lack of seat belt use, distraction, impairment, speeding, and drowsiness. We simply don't have the luxury of assuming driving automation will miraculously solve our transportation problems.

13. The Future of Transportation, Part III

How It Will Impact Users

I've saved one aspect of the automated-vehicle evolution for a chapter of its own. Here I want to consider how this technology will impact users in the real world.

Let's start with the money question. When new automotive technologies are introduced, they typically appear first in the most expensive luxury cars. This is because they cost a lot. As of today, you have to shell out big bucks for even a partially automated vehicle. Based on the manufacturer's suggested retail price (MSRP) data, model year 2019 vehicles with Level 2 driving automation cost around $80,000! The average price for a standard vehicle in the US is about $35,000. What is the likelihood of drivers spending $80,000 on a vehicle if they are used to paying only $35,000? Probably not that high. *Deloitte Review* recently found that drivers are hesitant to pay more money for advanced-vehicle systems. One reason for this may be that people are doing a cost-benefit analysis and they can't justify the added expense. A US Census Bureau report found that the average commute time to work is approximately 26 minutes, with about 25 percent of workers experiencing a commute time of 15 minutes or less. Do you want to spend $80,000 on a vehicle you'll only be in for a short amount of time each day?

At least for a while, the people most likely to be impacted by automated-vehicle technology are those with ample money to spend. In the long run, however, all of us will feel the impact as the most sophisticated automation technologies become increasingly integrated into our economy. For some, the impact will be negative. According to a 2017 WIRED article, some economists believe that industries reliant on drivers could lose about 300,000 jobs per year due to driving automation. This is an understandable concern if you're a truck driver; how many will be unemployed if truck fleets are automated?

Mobility for All?

Many advocates of automated and autonomous vehicles feel strongly that they will increase mobility across the board, including for people with disabilities and those in lower socioeconomic strata. Let's have a look at this claim.

In 2015 the US Department of Transportation released *Beyond Traffic 2045*, its strategic plan for where the nation's transportation system should head by 2045. The report points to a number of key challenges facing an aging transportation infrastructure that is struggling to keep pace with changes in technology, population, and climate:

- America's population will have grown by 70 million by 2045.
- By 2045 there will be nearly twice as many older Americans as now; they will need quality connections to medical care and related services.
- Between 5 and 10 million Americans are unable to drive because of disabilities.
- By 2050 emerging megaregions could absorb 75 percent of the US population while rural populations will continue declining.
- Freight volume will increase by more than 40 percent, driven in part by online shopping, adding extra demand to our transportation networks.
- Predicted rises in global temperatures and mean sea levels and more frequent and intense storm events could drastically affect highways, bridges, public transportation, coastal ports, and waterways.
- Low-income communities require special attention after years of neglect that has only intensified economic and racial segregation.

Not surprisingly, the report stresses the need for significant public investment to address these challenges, including the funding of transportation research and development, which can help us make difficult choices about how and where to invest limited resources wisely.

One area that receives particular attention in the report is automated-vehicle technology, which, the report claims, has the potential to be especially beneficial in addressing the needs of traditionally underserved communities, such as older drivers, those living in poor conditions, and persons with disabilities. From what you've now learned in this book, I hope you can see why the report makes this claim. At the same time you can also probably see why the challenge of making advanced transportation systems ubiquitous across all potential users is so daunting. For instance, automated vehicles could make a huge difference in addressing decades of neglect and discrimination in poor communities, but as the report points out, and as history tells us, underserved communities almost always lose out in the planning process. Will this change any time soon?

Addressing the needs of persons with disabilities presents its own unique challenges. Ever since the Americans with Disabilities Act became law in 1990, transit services have improved to comply with new standards—thus making transit more accessible to those with disabilities—but upwards of one-third of the 5 to 10 million US citizens with disabilities still find that their transportation options are inadequate. And as automation technologies are more widely adopted across the national population, governments must be prepared to address and mitigate the risks associated with increased reliance on ever more sophisticated and complex systems so that our transportation system remains safe, secure, and accessible.

A simple survey of current research being conducted on the transportation needs of persons with disabilities shows numerous areas that still require attention.

VTTI researchers in our Center for Vulnerable Road User Safety, including my colleagues Jon Antin and Justin Owens, have been examining the needs of people who are blind or visually impaired with respect to transportation network companies (think Uber). This is an area in which few studies have been conducted to date. For instance, network company drivers don't have to be trained to assist riders with special needs, so we are trying to determine the degree to which this lack of training affects the ability of Uber and Lyft to provide safe and reliable transportation options to these riders. This clearly becomes even more complex if we consider autonomous vehicles such as robotic taxis. Creating an autonomous shuttle that can meet the highly variable needs of persons with disabilities is perhaps at least as daunting as getting an autonomous vehicle to operate in the first place.

Other VTTI studies include assessing the general needs of drivers with autism, how persons with disabilities interact with advanced vehicles, how pedestrians with disabilities interact with advanced vehicles, and how senior drivers adapt to Level 2 and Level 3 automated vehicles. At the Center for

Advanced Transportation Mobility (CATM) of North Carolina A&T University, researchers are trying to determine the mobility needs of persons with disabilities, with the goal of reporting on current needs and challenges. The CATM folks are also doing research into mobility options for dialysis patients in North Carolina. While paratransit options specifically designed to transport dialysis patients to dialysis centers exist, they are not ubiquitous across all counties in the state due to lack of funding from the county government and decreasing support for health care services. If the paratransit options available now—which have their own set of challenges and shortcomings—aren't ubiquitously available, will the funding be there in the future to support automated paratransit options?

VTTI's newest automated vehicle is a low-speed, electric shuttle. It is being used initially to evaluate whether an automated shuttle system could improve public transportation access for vulnerable road users, such as the elderly and people with disabilities.

While the majority of these studies are ongoing, they will ultimately fill a current gap in knowledge about transportation options in relation to underserved communities. Yet, there are limitless other areas that need to be explored here. What are the mobility options, for instance, for persons with hearing loss, for amputees, for wheelchair users? What are the options for those with physical impairments (such as epilepsy, cerebral palsy, multiple sclerosis, spina bifida, or spinal cord injuries) or cognitive disabilities (such as Down syndrome, dementia, autism, or traumatic brain injuries)? How will transportation options in the years to come be made accessible to—and most importantly, *safe* for—these underserved individuals?

Ultimately, the message I want to leave you with is that automated vehicles have a tremendous amount of potential to benefit underserved communities, but we still have much to learn about how best to design and deploy these vehicles to safely and affordably meet individual needs. Even then, we must realize that automated vehicles aren't suddenly going to make everything better and give everyone equal opportunity to increased mobility.

Final Thoughts

Question What You Read and Hear

In some ways, driving safety is a funny business. Those of us in the business have our fair share of quirks. One thing you have to understand is that our data fluctuate, just as with many aspects of science. There are always new risks to analyze. New information continuously becomes available to enhance our current data. For instance, texting on a cell wasn't necessarily a risk even 10 years ago, and browsing on a cell wasn't even possible until a few years ago.

One particular stereotype of driving safety researchers is that we are somewhat risk averse since we deal with risk every day. Because of that, and because our data fluctuate and lives are on the line, we tend to be conservative in our thinking and writing. In general, therefore, we are not the best at getting information to you in a timely manner. Even when we are able to get the facts to you via an article or press release picked up by the media, the data may be presented in the wrong context or the main message we intended to convey wasn't there.

For example, when I was a young professor at the University of Idaho, my friend and very first graduate student, Jon Hankey, conducted a study with me that focused on fatigue when flying. (Jon is now the director of research and development for VTTI and had a huge role in getting our naturalistic driving data over the years.) This study looked at a pilot's ability to respond to an emergency situation after hours of mundane flight in a semi-sleep-deprived state. The pilots we recruited were kept awake for 24 hours. We then had them fly a simulator for two additional hours. It was an important study, revealing that pilots can recover pretty quickly and effectively when necessary. I was very excited, then, when the local paper came to do a story about our study. It was the first news article for my research. Jon and I talked to the reporter for about an hour, informing her of the merits and importance of our work.

At the very end of the discussion, the reporter said, "Wow, it must have been hard on the pilots to fly that simulator after being up all night." To which I responded, "Well, yes, it was a little bit of torture for them to get through it." The next day, with great anticipation, I stopped by a newspaper stand on the way to work. There was Jon and me with a caption that read, "UI Professor puts sleepy pilots through 'torture.'" Of course, I was shocked and dismayed, thinking my young career would soon end abruptly. In retrospect, though, we learned an important lesson and got a funny story out of it. To this day, Jon always prefers to delegate media interviews to our other researchers.

I want to finish with a story. In 2003 I received a call from a *Washington Post* reporter who was doing a story about an uptick in vehicle fatalities the previous year. An advocacy group called Public Citizen, which was founded by Ralph Nader, was advocating that the uptick was due to an increase in the number of SUVs on the road as well as the lack of rollover safety standards for SUVs. It turns out that regulatory agencies classified SUVs as pickup trucks, so SUVs did not have the same safety standards, such as roof-crush standards, as other passenger cars. The advocacy group had a worthy goal and an argument with some merit.

The reporter asked me if I thought the increase in fatalities was due to the lack of an SUV rollover standard. I replied that this might be one factor but that there were any number of other factors that might also contribute to an increase in the rate of fatal crashes. Moreover, any attempt to address the problem would almost certainly require a combination of high-tech responses (electronic stability control was being seriously considered at the time of the *Post* story) and low-tech responses (such as wearing seat belts and obeying the speed limit). The reporter then quoted me as saying, "You have to have all sorts of things to really make an impact these days [on the fatal crash rate]. The problems are getting harder to solve" and the solutions usually end up adding significantly to the cost or weight of a vehicle.

My statements made it into the *Post* story. However, one person clearly didn't like what I had said. Ralph Nader was also quoted toward the end of the piece dismissing my comments and those of others who were looking to find solutions through the use of active safety technology or crash avoidance technology. "Thirty years ago these guys were saying the same thing," Nader said. "These guys are incorrigible." The implication, of course, was that we were in the pocket of the car companies. After the *Post* story was published, my employer received a letter from Public Citizen accusing me of providing false statements and recommending that I be fired. None of this concerned me at the time. In fact, I took it as a point of pride and actually put a framed copy of the *Post* article on my wall.

What I've learned from incidents like these is that the driving safety industry is made up of both scientists and advocates—and they don't always see eye to eye. While I'm certain that the advocates mean well, they will occasionally cherry-pick or exaggerate what they want from scientific research to make a point. They tend to be politically savvy, and they will go to great lengths to make their advocacy issue matter even if it means ignoring or overlooking complexities in the scientific data. In this case, everything I said to the *Washington Post* reporter was correct, but I was "in the way" of the single ingredient that was being advocated. Ironically, I never disagreed with the merit of rollover standards for SUVs; I just didn't jump on the bandwagon and say that this was the one ingredient in the 2002 fatality rate increase.

This leads me to my final point. Much of what I've included here is grounded steadfastly in scientific fact, and some of it is on the cusp of being proven. At the same time, some of what you have read is my opinion based on studying and thinking about driving safety for more than 35 years. The majority of information is based on driving data that come from drivers actually driving in a real-world setting, as opposed to data from laboratory or simulator studies. These real-world driving studies offer a clear advantage: at this point in time, crash risk can't be estimated in the lab.

Some will inevitably disagree with aspects of this book. Others will misrepresent what I am trying to tell you by taking it out of context. Others still will claim that I lack sufficient data to draw meaningful conclusions about driving safety and, therefore, I really ought to keep my advice to myself. With this in mind, let me conclude by saying the following:

1. I may be wrong, but I am probably not.
2. At least I tried when others say we don't really know the answer about driving risks. To the contrary, I'm convinced we pretty much do know the answers.
3. Question anything you hear or read about driving safety in media reports, because I can guarantee you that much of it will be cherry-picked or inaccurate.
4. I will update you in the future through any means practical if I change my mind about what I've presented here, but don't expect there to be

too many updates.

Thanks for reading. Remember to stay alert and sober, stay away from trucks, and *keep your eyes on the road!*

References

AAA. "Aggressive Driving." https://bit.ly/2QwGREr.

AAA. "Digest of Motor Laws: Child Passenger Safety." https://drivinglaws.aaa.com/tag/child-passenger-safety/.

AAA. "Evaluate Your Driving Ability." http://seniordriving.aaa.com/evaluate-your-driving-ability.

AAA (2018). "Drivers Rely Too Heavily on New Vehicle Safety Technologies in Spite of Limitations." https://newsroom.aaa.com/2018/09/drivers-rely-heavily-new-vehicle-safety-technologies/.

AARP. http://www.aarp.org.

Andrey, J. (2010). "Long-Term Trends in Weather-Related Crash Risks." *Journal of Transport Geography* 18 (2): 247–58.

Bakalar, N. (2018). "Marijuana Use Tied to Fatal Car Crashes." *New York Times,* 4 April 2018. https://nyti.ms/2zQCPRO.

Ball, K., Berch, D. B., Helmers, K. F., Jobe, J. B., Leveck, M. D., Marsiske, M., ... & Unverzagt, F. W. (2002). "Effects of Cognitive Training Interventions with Older Adults: A Randomized Controlled Trial." JAMA 288 (18): 2271–81. http://www.ncbi.nlm.nih.gov/pmc/articles/PMC2916176/.

Blanco, M., Atwood, J., Vasquez, H. M., Trimble, T. E., Fitchett, V. L., Radlbeck, J., ... & Morgan, J. F. (2015). *Human Factors Evaluation of Level 2 and Level 3 Automated Driving Concepts* (Report No. DOT HS 812 182). Washington, DC: National Highway Traffic Safety Administration.

Blanco, M., Bocanegra, J. L., Morgan, J. F., Fitch, G. M., Medina, A., Olson, R. L., Hanowski, R. J., Daily, B., & Zimmermann, R. P. (2009). *Assessment of a Drowsy Driver Warning System for Heavy Vehicle Drivers: Final Report* (Report No. DOT HS 811 117). Washington, DC: National Highway Traffic Safety Administration.

Centers for Disease Control and Prevention (2019). "Child Passenger Safety:

Get the Facts." Last reviewed 13 September 2019. https://www.cdc.gov/motorvehiclesafety/child_passenger_safety/cps-factsheet.html.

Centers for Disease Control and Prevention (2019). "Drowsy Driving: Asleep at the Wheel." Last reviewed 7 November 2019. https://www.cdc.gov/features/dsdrowsydriving/index.html.

Centers for Disease Control and Prevention (2018). "Seat Belts: Get the Facts." Last reviewed 5 June 2018. http://www.cdc.gov/Motorvehiclesafety/seatbelts/facts.html.

Centers for Disease Control and Prevention (2019). "Teen Drivers: Get the Facts." Last reviewed 30 October 2019. https://www.cdc.gov/motorvehiclesafety/teen_drivers/teendrivers_factsheet.html.

Centers for Disease Control and Prevention (2017). "Rural Americans Less Likely to Wear Seat Belts, More Likely to Die in Crashes." https://www.cdc.gov/media/releases/2017/p0921-rural-seat-belts.html.

Centers for Disease Control and Prevention (2014). "CDC Report Shows Motor Vehicle Crash Injuries Are Frequent and Costly." http://www.cdc.gov/media/releases/2014/p1007-crash-injuries.html.

Crandall, C. S., Olson, L. M., & Sklar, D. P. (2001). "Mortality Reduction with Air Bag and Seat Belt Use in Head-On Passenger Car Collisions." *American Journal of Epidemiology* 153 (3): 219–24.

Curry, A. E., Pfeiffer, M. R., Durbin, D. R., Elliott, M. R., & Kim, K. H. (2015). "Young Driver Licensing: Examination of Population-Level Rates Using New Jersey's State Licensing Database." *Accident Analysis & Prevention* 76: 49–56.

Dingus, T. A., Owens, J. M., Guo, F., Fang, Y., Perez, M., McClafferty, J., Buchanan-King, M., Fitch, G. M. (in press). "The Prevalence of and Crash Risk Associated with Primarily Cognitive Secondary Tasks." *Safety Science*.

Dingus, T. (2017). "The Automated-Vehicle (R)evolution." Filmed October 2017. TEDx Wilmington Salon. https://youtu.be/uW-Xy8HOSUQ.

Dingus, T. A., Guo, F., Lee, S., Antin, J. F., Perez, M., Buchanan-King, M., & Hankey, J. (2016). "Driver Crash Risk Factors and Prevalence Evaluation

Using Naturalistic Driving Data." *Proceedings of the National Academy of Sciences* 113 (10): 2636–41. http://www.pnas.org/content/113/10/2636.

Dingus, T. A. (2014). "Estimates of Prevalence and Risk Associated with Inattention and Distraction Based Upon In Situ Naturalistic Data." *Annals of Advances in Automotive Medicine* 58: 60–68. http://www.ncbi.nlm.nih.gov/pmc/articles/PMC4001675/.

Dingus, T. A., McGehee, D. V., Manakkal, N., Jahns, S. K., Carney, C., & Hankey, J. (1997). "Human Factors Field Evaluation of Automotive Headway Maintenance/Collision Warning Devices." *Human Factors* 39 (2): 216–29.

Dingus, T. A., Hulse, M. C., McGehee, D. V., Manakkal, R., & Fleischman, R. N. (1994). "Driver Performance Results from the Travtek IVHS Camera Car Evaluation Study." *Proceedings of the Human Factors and Ergonomics Society Annual Meeting* 38 (17): 1118–22. https://doi.org/10.1177/154193129403801710.

Dingus, T. A., Hardee, H. L., & Wierwille, W. W. (1987). "Development of Models for On-Board Detection of Driver Impairment." *Accident Analysis & Prevention* 19 (4): 271–83. https://doi.org/10.1016/0001-4575(87)90062-5.

Dingus, T. A., Antin, J. F., Hulse, M. C., & Wierwille, W. W. (1986). *Human Factors Test and Evaluation of an Automobile Moving-Map Navigation System Part I: Attentional Demand Requirements.* Warren, MI: General Motors Research Laboratories.

Edmunds. http://www.edmunds.com.

Ehsani, J. P., Klauer, S. G., Zhu, C., Gershon, P., Dingus, T. A., & Simons-Morton, B. G. (2017). "Naturalistic Assessment of the Learner License Period." *Accident Analysis & Prevention* 106: 275–84. https://europepmc.org/articles/pmc5610634.

Fancher, P., Ervin, R., & Bogard, S. (1998). *A Field Operational Test of Adaptive Cruise Control System Operability in Naturalistic Use* (SAE Technical Paper No. 980852). https://doi.org/10.4271/980852.

Fancher, P., Ervin, R., Sayer, J., Hagan, M., Bogard, S., Bareket, Z., Mefford, M., & Haugen, J. (1997). *Intelligent Cruise Control Field Operational Test*

(Interim Report No. UMTRI-97–11). Ann Arbor: The University of Michigan Transportation Research Institute.

Farber, E. & Paley, M. (1993). "Using Freeway Traffic Data to Estimate the Effectiveness of Rear End Collision Countermeasures." Paper presented at the Third Annual IVHS America Meeting, IVHS America, Washington, DC.

Federal Highway Administration. "How Do Weather Events Impact Roads?" Last modified 20 February 2020. https://ops.fhwa.dot.gov/weather/q1_roadimpact.htm.

Federal Highway Administration. Our Nation's Highways: 2011. (2011). http://www.fhwa.dot.gov/policyinformation/pubs/hf/pl11028/chapter4.cfm.

Fitch, G. M., Soccolich, S. A., Guo, F., McClafferty, J., Fang, Y., Olson, R. L., ... & Dingus, T. A. (2013). The Impact of Hand-Held and Hands-Free Cell Phone Use on Driving Performance and Safety-Critical Event Risk (No. DOT HS 811 757). Washington, DC: National Highway Traffic Safety Administration.

Fung, B. (2017). "The Days of Owning a Car Could Be Fading Away, Thanks to These Alternatives." Washington Post, 20 March 2017. https://wapo.st/2ONi3Ln.

Garay Vega, L., Fisher, D. L., & Pollatsek, A. (2007). "Hazard Anticipation of Novice and Experienced Drivers: Empirical Evaluation on a Driving Simulator in Daytime and Nighttime Conditions." Transportation Research Record, 2009, 1–7.

Gellatly, A. W., & Dingus, T. A. (1998). "Speech Recognition and Automotive Applications: Using Speech to Perform In-Vehicle Tasks." Proceedings of the Human Factors and Ergonomics Society Annual Meeting 42 (17): 1247–51. https://doi.org/10.1177/154193129804201715.

Giffi, C., Vitale, J., Robinson, R., & Pingitore, G. (2017). "The Race to Autonomous Driving: Winning American Consumers' Trust." Deloitte Insights, 23 January 2017. https://bit.ly/2DWERAr.

Governors Highway Safety Association. "Motorcyclist Safety." http://www.ghsa.org/html/issues/motorcyclesafety.html.

Greenwell, N. K. (2015). *Results of the National Child Restraint Use Special Study* (Report No. DOT HS 812 142). Washington, DC: National Highway Traffic Safety Administration.

Hankey, J. M., McGehee, D. V., Dingus, T. A., Mazzae, E. N., & Garrott, W. R. (1996). "Initial Driver Avoidance Behavior and Reaction Time to an Unalerted Intersection Incursion." *Proceedings of the Human Factors and Ergonomics Society Annual Meeting* 40 (18): 896–99. https://doi.org/10.1177%2F154193129604001806.

Heads UP Georgia. "Hands-Free Law." http://www.headsupgeorgia.com/handsfree-law/.

HealthDay. "State Texting Bans Are Saving Teen Drivers' Lives." https://consumer.healthday.com/general-health-information-16/distracted-driving-968/state-texting-bans-are-saving-teen-drivers-lives-757673.html.

Hulse, M. C., Dingus, T. A., Fischer, T., & Wierwille, W. W. (1989). "The Influence of Roadway Parameters on Driver Perception of Attentional Demand." In *Advances in Industrial Ergonomics and Safety I*, edited by A. Mital, 451–56. New York: Taylor & Francis.

Ingraham, C. (2017). "What Marijuana Legalization Did to Car Accident Rates." *Washington Post*, 26 June 2017. https://wapo.st/2P8vLVW.

Ingraham, C. (2016). "The Astonishing Human Potential Wasted on Commutes." *Washington Post*, 25 February 2016. https://wapo.st/2AlLNGX.

Insurance Information Institute (2018). "Background On: Motorcycle Crashes." http://www.iii.org/issue-update/motorcycle-crashes.

Insurance Institute for Highway Safety. "Driver Death Rates by Make and Model." https://www.iihs.org/iihs/topics/driver-death-rates.

Insurance Institute for Highway Safety. "Graduated Licensing Calculator." https://www.iihs.org/topics/teenagers/gdl-calculator.

Insurance Institute for Highway Safety (2019). "Motorcycles." http://www.iihs.org/iihs/topics/t/motorcycles/fatalityfacts/motorcycles.

Insurance Institute for Highway Safety (2019). "Helmet Laws."

https://www.iihs.org/iihs/topics/laws/helmetuse/mapmotorcyclehel-mets.

Insurance Institute for Highway Safety (2018). "Choosing the Best Vehicle for Your Teen." https://www.iihs.org/iihs/ratings/vehicles-for-teens.

Insurance Institute for Highway Safety (2018). "IIHS Examines Driver Assistance Features in Road, Track Tests." 7 August 2018. https://www.iihs.org/news/detail/iihs-examines-driver-assistance-features-in-road-track-tests.

Insurance Institute for Highway Safety (2018). "Legal Pot: Crashes Are up in State with Retail Sales." *Status Report* 53, no. 6 (18 October 2018): 1–5. https://www.iihs.org/iihs/sr/statusreport/article/53/6/1.

Insurance Institute for Highway Safety (2017). "Stay within the Lines: Lane Departure Warning, Blind Spot Detection Help Drivers Avoid Trouble." *Status Report* 52, no. 6 (23 August 2017): 1–4. https://www.iihs.org/iihs/sr/statusreport/article/52/6/1.

Insurance Institute for Highway Safety (2017). "Lane Maintenance Systems Still a Turnoff for Many Drivers, New Observations Show." *Status Report* 52, no. 4 (22 June 2017): 6–7. https://www.iihs.org/iihs/sr/statusreport/article/52/4/3.

Insurance Institute for Highway Safety (2016). "Crashes Avoided: Front Crash Prevention Slashes Police-Reported Rear-End Crashes." *Status Report* 51, no. 1 (28 January 2016): 1–5. https://www.iihs.org/iihs/sr/statusreport/article/51/1/1.

Insurance Institute for Highway Safety (2016). "Life-Saving Benefits of ESC Continue to Accrue." *Status Report* 51, no. 7 (1 September 2016): 7. https://www.iihs.org/iihs/sr/statusreport/article/51/7/4.

Insurance Institute for Highway Safety (2016). *Status Report* 51, no. 8 (10 November 2016). https://www.aamva.org/IIHSReportAutVeh_Nov2016/.

Insurance Institute for Highway Safety (2016). "U.S. DOT and IIHS Announce Historic Commitment from 10 Automakers to Include Automatic Emergency Braking on All New Vehicles." 17 March 2016. https://www.iihs.org/news/detail/u-s-dot-and-iihs-announce-historic-commitment-of-20-automakers-to-make-automatic-emergency-braking-standard-on-new-vehicles.

Insurance Institute for Highway Safety (2014). "Eyes on the Road: Searching for Answers to the Problem of Distracted Driving." *Status Report* 49, no. 8 (24 October 2014): 1-6, 10-11. http://www.iihs.org/iihs/sr/statusreport/article/49/8/1.

Klauer, C., Ankem, G., Guo, F., Baynes, P., Fang, Y., Atkins, W., Baker, S., Duke, R., Hankey, J., & Dingus, T. (2017). *Driver Coach Study* (Report No. 17-UM-061). Blacksburg, VA: National Surface Transportation Safety Center for Excellence.

Klauer, S. G., Guo, F., Simons-Morton, B., Ouimet, M.C., Lee, S.E., & Dingus T. A. (2014). "Distracted Driving and Risk of Road Crashes among Novice and Experienced Drivers." *New England Journal of Medicine* 370: 54–59.

Knipling, R. R. (2004). *Individual Differences and the "High-Risk" Commercial Driver.* Vol. 4. Washington, DC: Transportation Research Board.

Li, K., Simons-Morton, B. G., Vaca, F. E., & Hingson, R. (2014). "Association between Riding with an Impaired Driver and Driving While Impaired." *Pediatrics* 144 (4): 620–26.

Lienert, P. (2018). "Most Americans Wary of Self-Driving Cars: Reuters/Ipsos Poll." *Reuters*, 28 January 2018. https://ca.reuters.com/article/technologyNews/idCAKBN1FI034-OCATC.

Lind, M., & Hensley, R. (2019). *Asymmetric Information Sharing in Dialysis Paratransit Using an Agency Approach (Abstract).* Greensboro: North Carolina A&T State University, Center for Advanced Transportation Mobility. https://www.ncat.edu/cobe/transportation-institute/catm/catm_documents/paratransit2finalreport-dec18.pdf

Marshall, A. (2017). "What Does Tesla's Automated Truck Mean for Truckers?" WIRED, 17 November 2017. https://www.wired.com/story/what-does-teslas-truck-mean-for-truckers/.

Masten, S. V., Foss, R. D., & Marshall, S. W. (2011). "Graduated Driver Licensing and Fatal Crashes Involving 16-to 19-Year-Old Drivers." JAMA 306 (10): 1098–103.

Miller, E. (2018). "Large-Truck Fatal Crashes up 3% in 2016, FMCSA Final Report Says." Transport Topics, 21 May 2018. https://www.ttnews.com/articles/large-truck-fatal-crashes-3-2016-fmcsa-final-report-says.

Mollenhauer, M., Dingus, T., Carney, C., Hankey, J., & Jahns, S. (1997). "Anti-Lock Brake Systems: An Assessment of Training on Driver Effectiveness." Accident Analysis & Prevention 29 (1): 97–108. https://doi.org/10.1016/S0001-4575(96)00065-6.

Motorcycle Safety Foundation. https://www.msf-usa.org/.

Motorcycle Safety Foundation (2006). Quick Tips: The Importance of Riding Unimpaired by Alcohol or Other Drugs. http://www.msf-usa.org/downloads/Alcohol_Awareness.pdf.

National Center for Injury Prevention and Control (2011). Policy Impact: Seat Belts. https://www.cdc.gov/motorvehiclesafety/pdf/policyimpact-seatbelts.pdf.

National Highway Traffic Safety Administration (2001). "Chapter 1: Introduction" (aggressive driving). In Evaluation of the Aggression Suppression Program, Milwaukee, Wisconsin. Washington, DC: National Highway Traffic Safety Administration. https://one.nhtsa.gov/people/injury/research/aggressionwisc/chapter_1.htm.

National Highway Traffic Safety Administration. "Drowsy Driving." https://www.nhtsa.gov/risky-driving/drowsy-driving.

National Highway Traffic Safety Administration. "Drunk Driving." https://www.nhtsa.gov/risky-driving/drunk-driving.

National Highway Traffic Safety Administration. "Fatality Analysis Reporting System (FARS)." http://www.nhtsa.gov/FARS.

National Highway Traffic Safety Administration. "Motorcycle Safety." https://www.nhtsa.gov/road-safety/motorcycle-safety.

National Highway Traffic Safety Administration. "Ratings." https://www.nhtsa.gov/ratings.

National Highway Traffic Safety Administration (2018). Seat Belt Use in 2017–Use Rates in the States and Territories (Report No. DOT HS 812 546).

Washington, DC: National Highway Traffic Safety Administration. https://crashstats.nhtsa.dot.gov/Api/Public/ViewPublication/812546.

National Highway Traffic Safety Administration (2018). *Speeding* (Report No. DOT HS 812 480). Washington, DC: National Highway Traffic Safety Administration. https://crashstats.nhtsa.dot.gov/Api/Public/ViewPublication/812480.

National Highway Traffic Safety Administration (2018). *Summary of Motor Vehicle Crashes* (Report No. DOT HS 812 580). Washington, DC: National Highway Traffic Safety Administration. https://crashstats.nhtsa.dot.gov/Api/Public/ViewPublication/812580.

National Highway Traffic Safety Administration (2018). "U.S. Department of Transportation Launches New Ad Campaign to Stop Impaired Driving." 14 August 2018. https://www.nhtsa.gov/press-releases/us-department-transportation-launches-new-ad-campaign-stop-impaired-driving.

National Highway Traffic Safety Administration (2017). *Alcohol-Impaired Driving* (Report No. DOT HS 812 450). Washington, DC: National Highway Traffic Safety Administration. https://crashstats.nhtsa.dot.gov/Api/Public/ViewPublication/812450.

National Highway Traffic Safety Administration (2017). "Manufacturers Make Progress on Voluntary Commitment to Include Automatic Emergency Braking on All New Vehicles." 21 December 2017. https://www.nhtsa.gov/press-releases/nhtsa-iihs-announcement-aeb.

National Highway Traffic Safety Administration (2017). "V2V Statement." 8 November 2017. https://www.nhtsa.gov/press-releases/v2v-statement.

National Highway Traffic Safety Administration (2016). *2015 Motor Vehicle Crashes: Overview* (Report No. DOT HS 812 318). Washington, DC: National Highway Traffic Safety Administration. https://crashstats.nhtsa.dot.gov/Api/Public/ViewPublication/812318.

National Highway Traffic Safety Administration (2015). *Drug and Alcohol Crash Risk* (Report No. DOT HS 812 117). Washington, DC: National Highway Traffic Safety Administration. https://www.nhtsa.gov/sites/nhtsa.dot.gov/files/812117-drug_and_alcohol_crash_risk.pdf.

National Highway Traffic Safety Administration (2014). *Driver License Compliance Status in Fatal Crashes* (Report No. DOT HS 812 046). Washington, DC: National Highway Traffic Safety Administration. https://crash-stats.nhtsa.dot.gov/Api/Public/ViewPublication/812046.

National Highway Traffic Safety Administration (2014). *Speeding* (Report No. DOT HS 812 021). Washington, DC: National Highway Traffic Safety Administration. http://www-nrd.nhtsa.dot.gov/Pubs/812021.pdf.

National Highway Traffic Safety Administration (2013). *2012 Motor Vehicle Crashes: Overview* (Report No. DOT HS 811 856). Washington, DC: National Highway Traffic Safety Administration. http://www-nrd.nhtsa.dot.gov/Pubs/811856.pdf.

National Highway Traffic Safety Administration (2012). *Quick Facts 2012.* Washington, DC: National Highway Traffic Safety Administration. http://www-nrd.nhtsa.dot.gov/Pubs/812006.pdf.

National Highway Traffic Safety Administration (2009). *Seat Belt Use in 2008–Demographic Results* (Report No. DOT HS 811 183). Washington, DC: National Highway Traffic Safety Administration. https://crash-stats.nhtsa.dot.gov/Api/Public/ViewPublication/811183.

National Highway Traffic Safety Administration (1984). *Amendment to Federal Motor Vehicle Safety Standard Number 208: Passenger Car Front Seat Occupant Protection* (Federal Regulatory Impact Analysis). Washington, DC: National Highway Traffic Safety Administration. http://www-nrd.nhtsa.dot.gov/pubs/806572.pdf.

National Sleep Foundation. "Teens and Sleep." http://sleepfoundation.org/sleep-topics/teens-and-sleep.

Neale, V. L., Klauer, S. G., Knipling, R. R., Dingus, T. A., Holbrook, G. T., & Petersen, A. (2002). *The 100 Car Naturalistic Driving Study: Phase I-Experimental Design* (No. HS 809 536). Washington, DC: National Highway Traffic Safety Administration.

Neale, V. L., Dingus, T. A., Garness, S. A., Keisler, A. S., & Carroll, R. J. (2002). "The Relationship between Truck Driver Sleeper Berth Sleep Quality and

Safety-Related Critical Events." In *Proceedings of the Third International Truck and Bus Safety Research and Policy Symposium*, 65–78.

Olson, R. L., Hanowski, R. J., Hickman, J. S., & Bocanegra, J. (2009). *Driver Distraction in Commercial Vehicle Operations* (No. FMCSA-RRT-09-042). Washington, DC: Federal Motor Carrier Safety Administration.

OneDUI Insurance. "Costs for DUI." http://onedui.com/dui-costs/.

Owens, J. *Analysis of the Non-Driving Mobility Needs of People with Disabilities (Abstract)*. Greensboro: North Carolina A&T State University, Center for Advanced Transportation Mobility. https://www.ncat.edu/cobe/transportation-institute/catm/catm-finalreport_disability-survey_final-1.pdf

Owens, J. M., Dingus, T. A., Guo, F., Fang, Y., Perez, M., McClafferty, J., & Tefft, B. C. (2018). *Estimating the Prevalence and Crash Risk of Drowsy Driving Using Data from a Large-Scale Naturalistic Driving Study* (No. 18-04410). Washington, DC: AAA Foundation for Traffic Safety.

Pedbikeinfo. "Safety." https://bit.ly/1NvgoB2.

Pradhan, A. K., Pollatsek, A., Knodler, M., & Fisher, D. L. (2009). "Can Younger Drivers Be Trained to Scan for Information That Will Reduce Their Risk in Roadway Traffic Scenarios That Are Hard to Identify as Hazardous?" *Ergonomics* 52: 657–73.

Radcliffe, S. (2017). "Does Marijuana Increase the Risk of Vehicle Crashes?" Healthline, 27 June 2017. https://bit.ly/2y7clun.

Rebok, G. W., Ball, K., Guey, L. T., Jones, R. N., Kim, H. Y., King, J. W., ... & Willis, S. L. (2014). "Ten-Year Effects of the ACTIVE Cognitive Training Trial on Cognition and Everyday Functioning in Older Adults." *Journal of the American Geriatrics Society* 62 (1): 16–24. http://www.ncbi.nlm.nih.gov/pmc/articles/PMC4055506/.

Romoser, M. R. E., Pollatsek, A., Fisher, D. L., & Williams, C. C. (2013). "Comparing the Glance Patterns of Older Versus Younger Experienced Drivers: Scanning for Hazards While Approaching and Entering the Intersection." *Transportation Research Part F* 16 (January): 104–16.

SAE International (2018). *Taxonomy and Definitions for Terms Related to Driving Automation Systems for On-Road Motor Vehicles.* https://www.sae.org/standards/content/j3016_201806.

Safety Through Disruption (Safe-D) University Transportation Center. *Examining Senior Drivers Adaptation to Level 2–3 Automated Vehicles: A Naturalistic Study* (2019). https://www.vtti.vt.edu/utc/safe-d/index.php/projects/examining-senior-drivers-adaptation-to-level-2-3-automated-vehicles-a-naturalistic-study/.

Safety Through Disruption (Safe-D) University Transportation Center. *Older Drivers and Transportation Network Companies: Investigating Opportunities for Increased Safety and Improved Mobility* (2019). https://www.vtti.vt.edu/utc/safe-d/index.php/projects/older-drivers-and-transportation-network-companies-investigating-opportunities-for-increased-safety-and-improved-mobility/.

Safety Through Disruption (Safe-D) University Transportation Center. *Safety Perceptions of Transportation Network Companies (TNCs) by the Blind and Visually Impaired (BVI)* (2018). https://www.vtti.vt.edu/utc/safe-d/index.php/projects/safety-perceptions-of-transportation-network-companies-tncs-by-the-blind-and-visually-impaired-bvi/.

Sayer, J., Devonshire, J. M., & Flannagan, C. (2005). *The Effects of Secondary Task Performance on Naturalistic Driving* (Technical report No. UMTRI-2005-29). Ann Arbor: University of Michigan Transportation Research Institute.

Simons-Morton, B. G., Ouimet, M. C., Zhang, Z., Klauer, S. E., Lee, S. E., Wang, J., ... & Dingus, T. A. (2011). "The Effect of Passengers and Risk-Taking Friends on Risky Driving and Crashes/Near Crashes Among Novice Teenagers." *Journal of Adolescent Health* 49 (6): 587–93. http://www.ncbi.nlm.nih.gov/pmc/articles/PMC3218800/.

Sivak, M., & Schoettle, B. (2015). *Motion Sickness in Self-Driving Vehicles* (Report No. UMTRI-2015-12). Ann Arbor: University of Michigan Transportation Research Institute.

Staedter, T. (2017). "With Legal Pot, Fatal Car Crashes Haven't Increased." Live Science, 22 June 2017. https://bit.ly/2Oysqme.

State Farm (2018). "Chances of Hitting a Deer in My State." https://newsroom.statefarm.com/2018-deer-crashes-down/.

Statista (2017). "Total Number of Licensed Drivers in the U.S. in 2017, by State." https://www.statista.com/statistics/198029/total-number-of-us-licensed-drivers-by-state/.

Taub, E. A. (2018). "2-Second Rule for Distracted Driving Can Mean Life or Death." *New York Times*, 27 September 2018. https://nyti.ms/2zDgRSs.

Tefft, B. C., Williams, A. F., & Grabowski, J. G. (2013). *Timing of Driver's License Acquisition and Reasons for Delay among Young People in the United States, 2012*. Washington, DC: AAA Foundation for Traffic Safety.

Tesla (2018). "An Update on Last Week's Accident." Tesla blog, 30 March 2018. https://www.tesla.com/blog/update-last-week%E2%80%99s-accident.

Thomas, F. D., Korbelak, K. T., Divekar, G. U., Blomberg, R. D., Romoser, M. R. E., & Fisher, D. L. (2013). *Evaluation of a New Approach to Training Hazard Anticipation Skills of Young Drivers*. Washington, DC: National Highway Traffic Safety Administration.

Trivedi, T. K., Liu, C., Antonio, A. L. M., et al. (2019). "Injuries Associated with Standing Electric Scooter Use." *JAMA Network Open* 2 (1): 1–9. https://doi.org/10.1001/jamanetworkopen.2018.7381.

University of Minnesota (2014). "Students' Grades and Health Improve with Later High School Start Times." 12 March 2014. https://twincities.umn.edu/news-events/students-grades-and-health-improve-later-high-school-start-times.

US Department of Labor. "Office of Disability Employment Policy (ODEP)." https://www.dol.gov/odep/.

US Department of Transportation. *Beyond Traffic 2045*. https://www.transportation.gov/sites/dot.gov/files/docs/BeyondTraffic_tagged_508_final.pdf.

US Department of Transportation (2018). UTC *Spotlight* (No. 119). https://mycutc.com/wp-content/uploads/2018/02/utcnewsletterfebruary2018508.pdf.

Virginia Tech Transportation Institute (2018). "Teen Crash Risk Highest During First Three Months After Getting Driver's License." https://www.vtti.vt.edu/featured/?p=931.

Vlek, C., & Stallen, P. J. (1981). "Judging Risks and Benefits in the Small and in the Large." *Organizational Behavior and Human Performance* 28: 235–71.

WSAV (2018). "Report: GA Hands-Free Law Decreases Traffic Fatalities, Insurance Claims." 15 October 2018. https://www.wsav.com/news/local-news/georgia-news/report-ga-hands-free-law-decreases-traffic-fatalities-insurance-claims/1525388543.

Illustration Credits

Unless otherwise indicated, all illustrations are courtesy of Tom Dingus or the Virginia Tech Transportation Institute.

Figure 2. Photo by Tablexxnx. (CC BY-SA 2.0). (2016). Highway. Retrieved from https://www.flickr.com/photos/tablexxnx/24599911119/in/photolist-DtNYwB-DX8CA2-pTYqCx-5Cpj85-9zqX5U-2rMja7-ez37ox-816C9d-PGzXmk-EVy5-51pcog-iNS6F-MbbGxJ-8fwKVZ-5hB12E-4yEh3p-8fA2Bh-2m veEx-5CpiSu-e3Y5LJ-83wRQA-4yJxRm-bB2w1-KTyGg-nXwicZ-4yEh86-8udouo-qLVYv-6H7SHC-aLAZWV-RuRSgi-RuRToP-bFeVpw-RrgMN7-MCWS2W-K5Ewhk-h332u5-LtTc8J-84XHMb-Dms2wG-8f wJai-66qJRS-aM4SjB-9usM34-4FfvyX-K6SGBe-4kxymz-R8LWoy-8KssSp-cBJGeC

Figure 4. Photo from Dreamstime stock image library

Figure 5a. Photo by William Frye. (CC BY CC0 1.0). (2017). Highway Patrol Officer Cpl. Micheal Elkins assists Alabama National Guard Soldiers as they clear stranded traffic on Hwy. 59, Birmingham, Alabama. Retrieved from https://commons.wikimedia.org/wiki/File:Alabama_High-way_Patrol_assisting_Alabama_National_Guard_during_win-ter_storm_(1-4).jpg

Figure 5b. Photo from Global Center for Automotive Performance Simulation.

Figure 6. Car Seat Safety Advertisement by NDDOT. (CC BY CC0 1.0). (2018). Car Seat Safety. Retrieved from https://www.flickr.com/photos/nddot/45218983462

Figure 8. Photo by Prayitno Hadinata. (CC BY 2.0). (2011). LA traffic jam = daily occurrence !. Retrieved from https://www.flickr.com/photos/prayitnopho-tography/6806878281/

Figure 9. Photo by Ellery. (CC BY-SA 4.0). (2017). Blind Spot Indicator of 2016 Ford Focus 1.5T. Retrieved from https://commons.wikimedia.org/wiki/

File:Blind_Spot_Indicator-2016_Ford_Focus_1.5T_(mark_3.5)-DSC_1455.jpg

Figure 12. Photo by TruckTrend. (CC BY CC0 1.0). (2015). Royal Truck & Equipment Showcases Autonomous TMA Concept. Retrieved from http://www.trucktrend.com/news/1508-royal-truck-and-equipment-showcases-autonomous-tma-concept.

Figure 13. Photo by Logan Wallace

Figure 14. Photo from Oregon Department of Transportation. (CC BY 2.0). (2008). Snow and ice conditions. Retrieved from https://www.flickr.com/photos/oregondot/5124402104/

Figure 15a. Photo by MrX. (CC BY-SA 3.0). (2008). Key Deer on Deer Key. Retrieved from https://commons.wikimedia.org/wiki/File:Key_Deer_on_Deer_Key.jpg

Figure 16. Photo by Michel Curi. (CC BY 2.0). (2014). ChiTown Friday Night. Retrieved from https://commons.wikimedia.org/wiki/File:ChiTown_Friday_Night_(14684244008).jpg.

Figure 17b. Photo by Juliancolton. (CC BY CC0 1.0). (2009). Looking down a rural dirt road after a bout of snowfall in Dutchess County, New York, USA. Retrieved from https://commons.wikimedia.org/wiki/File:Dirt_road_in_winter.JPG

Figure 19a. Photo by Andrew Bossi. (CC-BY-SA-2.5). (2006). MD 124 (Mid-county Highway) at Goshen Road, Gaithersburg, MD, USA. Retrieved from https://commons.wikimedia.org/wiki/File:2006_12_15_-_124@Goshen_-_EB_06.JPG

Figure 20. Photo from CSPAN

Figure 21. Photo by Scott L. (CC BY-SA 2.0). (2014). An officer with the Los Angeles Police Department checks the sobriety of a driver in Hollywood over the Memorial Day weekend. Retrieved from https://commons.wikimedia.org/wiki/File:LAPD_Memorial_Day_Checkpoint.jpg

Figure 24. Public domain photo

Figure 25. Still from the movie Groundhog Day, Copyright © 1993, Columbia Pictures

Figure 26. Photo by Kgbo. (CC BY-SA 4.0). (2019). LimeBike scooters in Brisbane, Queensland October 2019. Retrieved from https://commons.wikimedia.org/wiki/
File:LimeBike_scooters_in_Brisbane,_Queensland,_October_2019.jpg

Figure 27. Photo by Jim.henderson. (CC BY CC0 1.0). (2009). Looking south from 30th Street at bike lane in 9th Ave on a cloudy afternoon. Retrieved from https://commons.wikimedia.org/wiki/File:Bikelane_9Av_30_jeh.JPG

Figure 28. VTTI chart as based on findings from Simons-Morton et al. (2011)

Figure 32. Photo by Fuchs Robert. (CC BY 3.0). (2016). Stilfserjoch-Passo dello Stelvio. Retrieved from https://commons.wikimedia.org/wiki/File:Stilfserjoch-Passo_dello_Stelvio_-_panoramio_-_Fuchs_Robert_(10).jpg

Figure 34. Public domain photo

Figure 36. Photo by TedX Salon

Figure 37. Photo by Marc dan der Chijs. (CC BY-ND 2.0). (2015). Testing the Tesla autopilot (self driving mode). Retrieved from https://www.flickr.com/photos/chijs/22274503931/in/photolist-
dtNMk2-KSVnz5-9M2QU4-AMT3Ne-zT6hwJ-oorCEE-zWjDZe-eAEQoD-
okV4hS-6FxgTr-Fnc15o-FnbXbs-Gfm7Po-Gfm7CG-G9tVGQ-GbMR1r-GbMS
e8-GhD21n-FSwEH9-GbMRjx-FnnkQp-GbMQzg-GhD2Gx-GbMPEa-
G9tT6C-GbMP6p-Gfm5G7-GbMQsc-FnbXK3-GbMQhn-G9tTKJ-FnnoiR-
Gfm8KS-FnbYyh-Gfm7kY-Gfm8H7-FSwDu7-G9tVAs-GbMRAK-GbMPCX-FS
wEF5-Gfm7qY-G9tU7q-FnnmXz-GhD1Ti-GbMPTX-Fnnoun-JbAC7z-
dYz4sg-2fB64wL

Figure 38. Photo by Ich. (CC BY-SA 3.0). (2012). Drunk driving simulator, Montreal by CAA of Quebec. Retrieved from:https://commons.wikimedia.org/wiki/File:Drunk_driving_simulator,_Montreal_by_CAA_of_Quebec.jpg

Figure 39. Photo from IIHS

Figure 40. Photo by Екатерина Волкова. (CC BY-SA 2.0). (2019). Self-Driving

Car Yandex.Taxi. Retrieved from https://commons.wikimedia.org/wiki/ File:Self-Driving_Car_Yandex.Taxi.jpg

Figure 41. Photo from Virginia Tech Daily. (2019). VTTI's newest automated vehicle is a low-speed, electric EasyMile EZ10 shuttle. Retrieved from https://vtnews.vt.edu/articles/2019/05/053019-vtti-autonomousshuttle.html

About the Authors

Dr. Tom Dingus has been conducting transportation safety research for more than 35 years. He is director of the Virginia Tech Transportation Institute (VTTI), which is home to the largest group of driving safety researchers in the world. In collaboration with VTTI researchers and engineers, Dr. Dingus has pioneered the naturalistic driving study research method and is working to ensure the safe development and deployment of the next generation of vehicular technology.

Mindy Buchanan-King is a project associate at VTTI. For the past 11 years, she has turned "engineer-speak" into impactful articles and award-winning publications.

Made in the USA
Columbia, SC
14 December 2020